Brian

T0270187

111 Places
in Hollywood
That You Must
Not Miss

emons:

For my mom and dad, who know that Hollywood is a beautiful neighborhood where actual people grow up, fall in love, and make families. Not at all like a story in a movie.

© Emons Verlag GmbH
© Photographs by Brian Joseph, except see p. 238
© Cover Icon: Istockphoto.com/wellesenterprises
Layout: Editorial Design & Art Direction, Conny Laue,
based on a design by Lübbeke | Naumann | Thoben
Maps: velovia, www.velovia.bike
Frank Ullrich & Kristof Halasz
© OpenStreetMap contributors
Editing: Karen E. Seiger
Printing and binding: Grafisches Centrum Cuno, Calbe
Printed in Germany 2023
ISBN 978-3-7408-1819-7
First edition

Guidebooks for Locals & Experienced Travelers
Join us in uncovering new places around the world at
www.111places.com

Foreword

I always thought that Hollywood was an idea, not a place. Tinseltown! A glittering dream of fame and glamor; a story of an attractive young superstar, perhaps, bursting with charisma and about to be discovered. There's a dark side to the mythology, too. Marilyn Monroe famously said, "Hollywood is a place where they'll pay you a thousand dollars for a kiss and fifty cents for your soul. I know, because I turned down the first offer often enough and held out for the fifty cents." Alas, Marilyn. So many Hollywood stories have ended tragically. This false binary notion formed my thoughts about Hollywood. It's all or nothing, boom or bust.

But this simplistic and wrong idea leaves out two facts that made me fall in love with this vibrant, diverse, one-of-a-kind place. Firstly, people *live* here. Tens of thousands of them! I wanted to capture the fun and thrill of Hollywood, but also tell stories of the history, from the Indigenous Tongva people who inhabited it for centuries, all the way through resettlement, redlining, and redemption. Yes, there are stories about fame, of course. Many tragic stories too. But there's so much more to the Hollywood tapestry than just the fringes.

Secondly, my parents grew up here. My mother lived in a modest house in Hollywood that was displaced to put in a freeway (damn it, Los Angeles, you and your stupid cars). My father had his Bar Mitzvah at Temple Israel of Hollywood, in the very sanctuary that I photographed for this book.

I hope you'll get a sense of how much fun it was for me to visit not only some of Hollywood's most iconic spots, like the Griffith Park Observatory or the Musso & Frank Grill, but also some secret spots that are literally tucked away in backyards, like the Was Ist Das? cabaret, the Hollywood Sculpture Garden, or the Birdhouse. Most of all, I hope you'll come visit Hollywood again and again.

111 Places

1 American Legion Post 43

Honoring veterans of all eras

They call it, "The Post of the Stars," and it's a very fitting name. Veterans who were working in the entertainment industry chartered the Hollywood chapter of the American Legion way back in 1919. Clark Gable, Gene Autry, and Charlton Heston were all members in their time, as well as countless other Hollywood luminaries who served in the armed forces. The American Legion's mission of taking care of veterans is consistent across locations around the country. But there's no place that does it with as much panache as the Hollywood Post 43.

The beautiful, 30,000 square-foot clubhouse of Post 43 was built in 1929 in the Egyptian Revival style, and when you enter past the stunning exterior, it feels like you've stepped back into another era. In 1989, the building was designated as a historic-cultural monument, and it's easy to see why. The Art Deco bar, once a speakeasy where Humphrey Bogart was a regular, Cabaret Room banquet hall, the gorgeous Rotunda and Trophy Room all make this place live up to the moniker, "The coolest private club in town." Veterans and service members from every era can meet here, play and relax together, and find community.

Non-veterans are welcome here too, and there are many ways to get involved. The American Legion is a nonprofit, so donations are tax deductible and very much appreciated, as they help the Legion continue doing its good work of supporting veterans, service members, and their families. The American Legion Auxiliary, Sons of the Legion, and American Legion Riders are all ways for Veterans' families and loved ones to participate and contribute to charitable causes of all kinds, including helping schools and hospitals, offering scholarships, and so much more. Hollywood Post 43 has also become the go-to place for film screenings and concerts, and most of the gorgeous refurbished spaces can be rented for private events.

Address 2035 N Highland Avenue, Hollywood, CA 90068, +1 (323) 851-3030, www.hollywoodpost43.org | **Getting there** Metro B to Hollywood/Highland (Red Line) | **Hours** See website for events | **Tip** The Hollywood Legion Stadium, owned by the American Legion, was one of Los Angeles' main boxing arenas in the 1920s and the vintage building, now leased to LA Fitness, is still there (1628 El Centro Avenue).

2 __ Andaz Hyatt

Welcome to the Riot House

Tales of the crazy antics of rock bands from the 1970s are plentiful. Drug and alcohol-fueled debauchery, outrageous parties, and naked groupies. It's all part of the lore and legend of rock 'n' roll. Some of it is even true. Many of the places where the craziest stuff happened are, of course, right here in Hollywood. The Continental Hyatt House hotel got the nickname "The Riot House" because of its reputation for wildness.

Opened in 1963 by the beloved singing cowboy, the hotel was known for a time as the Gene Autry Hotel. It was sold to Hyatt in 1966 and quickly gained a reputation as the place to stay for hard-partying rockers. It's next to several record labels, and legendary clubs like the Whisky, the Roxy, and the Troubadour. So it was a perfect place for bands like The Who and The Rolling Stones, who were regulars. Keith Moon and Keith Richards both tossed televisions out the windows here. When Led Zeppelin was in town, the band would reportedly rent out as many as six floors of the hotel to make room for the decadent all-nighters. Did John Bonham really ride a motorcycle down the hallway? Yup, he sure did. The band learned to bring an accountant along on tours to keep track of damages, and the hotel took a $50,000 deposit when they stayed.

Little Richard lived here for a time. So did Jim Morrison, but he was evicted after dangling from a 10th-story window above Sunset Boulevard. Nude football games were played in the hallways, huge orgies spilled from room to room. Movies like *Almost Famous* and *Strange Days* recreated some of the craziest moments from those hedonistic years.

The hotel is now the Andaz West Hollywood, and the crazy days seem to be mostly in the past. You can enjoy the beautiful rooftop pool, or even rent an entire floor if you can afford it. But the TVs are bolted down now, and you'll have to leave your Harley outside.

Address 8401 Sunset Boulevard, West Hollywood, CA 90069, +1 (323) 656-1234 | Getting there Bus 2 to Sunset/Kings | Hours Unrestricted | Tip Soak up some more classic Hollywood vibes by checking out the famous Chateau Marmont, where Bonham also rode his Harley down the hall (8221 Sunset Boulevard, www.chateaumarmont.com).

3 Artisan's Patio

Hollywood's last wishing well

The sign in front of the Artisan's Patio has this simple yet intriguing proclamation: *15 Unusual Shops*. While that's a true statement, this is a much more special place than that humble advertisement makes it sound. It's also not surprising that it isn't too well known, as this little historic gem is very easy to miss. A narrow iron gate opens into a little pedestrian avenue connected to the only remaining "courtyard building" on Hollywood Boulevard. This is why, in 1989, the Artisan's Patio was certified as an official LA historic-cultural monument. Look for the official plaque commemorating the designation just inside the gate.

Walking into this charming patio feels a bit like going back in time. After all, this place is more or less the same as it was when it was built in 1918. A series of small, unassuming shops surround an old wishing well, which is like nothing else in town. The design of the building itself is simply wonderful, having been imagined by architects Octavius Morgan and John Walls, the same team that built such Los Angeles landmarks as the Mayan Theatre, the Wiltern Theatre, and many more buildings that stand out, even in a city full of standouts. It's easy to imagine this building a century ago, when nearby movie studios were abuzz with the strivings of a popular new industry, and little courtyards such as this one dotted the boulevard. Which stars of the Golden Age may have slipped through this thin gate to enjoy this shady courtyard?

What are the "unusual shops" hidden in the Artisan's Patio? Well, it changes from time to time, of course, and that's part of the fun of visiting. In recent years, there's been a record store, a store for Hollywood memorabilia, an African gift shop, a guitar repair shop and many more. One thing is certain – duck into this courtyard, and you're entering into a little corner of Hollywood history.

Address 6729 Hollywood Boulevard, Hollywood, CA 90028 | Getting there Metro B to Hollywood/Highland (Red Line) | Hours Variable, usually regular business hours | Tip Art lovers will enjoy the Kohn Gallery for pop art and modern exhibitions (1227 N Highland Avenue, www.kohngallery.com).

4 Awards Walk

How many Oscar winners have you seen?

The most celebrated red carpet in Hollywood is undoubtedly outside the Dolby Theatre on the evening of the Academy Awards. If you've been nominated for an Oscar, you already know how special it is. You waded through the phalanx of press, showed off your outfit and answered some interview questions, and then made your way into the beautiful theater, where the Oscars have been held since 2001. There, amidst all the glitz and glamour, you discovered the Awards Walk, a display of beautifully backlit glass plaques featuring every single Best Picture Oscar winner. You ascended a grand staircase, where you reminisced about your favorite films as you viewed the titles, nestled here in limestone portals on two floors of the theater. Dazzled by the display, you entered to find your seat for the ceremony. Truly an exquisite way to enjoy a delightful place.

The second-best way to enjoy the Awards Walk is to just show up on almost any other day of the year. You're still welcome to wear your fancy threads (this is Hollywood, after all), but odds are good that you won't be bothered by paparazzi as you make your way through the grand portal to the theater. Stroll through film history, from the very first winner, 1927's *Wings*, through dozens of other memorable films, like *Casablanca* (1943), *On the Waterfront* (1954), *The Godfather* (1972), and so many other great movies.

Of course, it's not the only reason to go. The Dolby Theatre has a full array of big concerts, Broadway musicals, and special events lined up all year round. Unsurprisingly, the Dolby has one of the most sophisticated sound systems of any theater in the world. In addition to the Oscar winners, the lobby of the theater has five floors, all filled with photos, memorabilia, and more. Most people enjoy strolling through the Awards Walk and counting the number of Oscar-winners they've seen, and the ones they have not.

Address 6801 Hollywood Boulevard, Hollywood, CA 90028, +1 (323) 308-6300, www.dolbytheatre.com | Getting there Metro B to Hollywood/Highland (Red Line) | Hours See website | Tip For a deeper dive into the Academy Awards, visit the Academy Museum of Motion Pictures (6067 Wilshire Boulevard, www.academymuseum.org).

5 Barnsdall Art Park

Hollywood's World Heritage Site

In order to be selected as a World Heritage Site, The United Nations Educational, Scientific and Cultural Organization (UNESCO) has to determine that a place has such a significant "cultural… [or] natural heritage" that it is "considered to be of outstanding value to humanity." There are three places in all of California that have met this high standard. The first two are national parks: Yosemite, one of the world's most spectacular natural wonders, and Redwood National Park, home to some of the oldest and grandest trees on the planet. The third? Well, it's in Hollywood at the amazing eleven and a half acres that make up the Barnsdall Art Park.

It may seem like a surprising accolade for a small city park, but consider that the Barnsdall Art Park features the Los Angeles Municipal Art Gallery, which has been solely exhibiting art since 1954, making it the longest running institution to do so in all of Los Angeles. There's also the Barnsdall Gallery Theatre, a gorgeous, 300-seater featuring all kinds of cultural events, not to mention an art center that offers adult and youth classes. Still not convinced? Then please note that the park is filled with architectural wonders. Several of the stunning buildings were designed by renowned architect Richard Neutra.

In actuality, though, UNESCO singled out Barnsdall for the World Heritage distinction because the park is also the site of The Hollyhock House, designed a century ago by Frank Lloyd Wright. Hollyhock was the very first of his Los Angeles commissions, and it became a catalyst for the modern California architecture movement. With Mayan accents outside and distinctive, stylized representations of the Hollyhock plant inside, it isn't surprising that UNESCO determined that this gem was worth celebrating and preserving. It's the only Wright house that is open to the public and well worth a visit.

Address 4800 Hollywood Boulevard, Hollywood, CA 90027, +1 (323) 644-6296, www.barnsdall.org, barnsdallartpark@lacity.org | Getting there Metro B to Vermont/ Sunset (Red Line) | Hours Daily 6am–10pm | Tip There are several Frank Lloyd Wright homes in Hollywood, and one of them, the Ennis House, is only a mile and a half away (2655 Glendower Avenue, www.franklloydwright.org/site/ennis-house).

6 The Batcave

Holy headless horror!

Early one sunny morning in 2012, professional dog walker Lauren Kornberg was strolling past the iconic Bronson Caves with her mother and eight friendly dogs. Her golden retriever Ollie scampered into the brush and came out with a plastic shopping bag. At that moment, out of the bag rolled a freshly decapitated human head. Only in Hollywood!

"The Hollywood Head," as it came to be known, turned out to belong to the unfortunate Hervey Medellin. He was murdered somewhere else, but, in what sounds like a grisly twist from one of the numerous crime shows that have been filmed here, this is where his head and hands wound up being dumped.

Known by locals as The Batcave, the Bronson Caves have been featured in over five thousand movies and tv shows, astonishingly, including the original *Batman*, *The Lone Ranger*, *Zorro*, *Wonder Woman*, *Twin Peaks* and countless others. It's called the Bronson Caves after a nearby street that also lent itself as Charles Bronson's (born Charles Buchinsky) last name.

The man-made cave is actually a short tunnel that was part of a quarry at the turn of the 20th century, where crushed rock was excavated to pave the streets of Hollywood. It's safe to explore, short enough that you don't even need a flashlight, and there are *almost* never any severed heads found here. At the back of the cave, you'll want to take a selfie, and then turn around for a great view of the Hollywood Sign and the beautiful hills of Griffith Park.

The "Batcave" is still used quite regularly for filming, but most days it's simply an idyllic stroll up a gentle trail. It's less than a mile round trip, and only about a 50-foot rise in elevation, so it's an easy walk for most. As Lauren and the other pros will tell you, "It's a great place for walking dogs, and if they should wander off the trail, just beware of any suspicious things they might find and drop at your feet."

Address 3200 Canyon Drive, Hollywood, CA 90068, www.laparks.org/park/bronson-canyon | Getting there By car, drive through the south side of the park to the end of Canyon Drive, then walk up the hill and take a right at the little road behind the red metal gate. Follow the path up around the turn to the caves. | Hours Daily 5am–10:30pm | Tip Now that you've seen the Batcave, head over to Golden Apple Comics to keep the superhero vibe alive (7018 Melrose Avenue, www.goldenapplecomics.com).

7 The BirdHouse

Restoration of land and people

Much of the world's population lives in densely populated cities. There are some conveniences, but when you pour concrete over the natural environment and plop a few million people down on top of it, some major problems can develop as well. People disconnect from one another, the once fertile land becomes largely dry and barren, and communities are mostly getting food, medicine, and arts and culture from distant sources. John Allen and Bella LeNestour were troubled by these realities, and in 2016, they decided to try and make some changes in their Hollywood community. The result of their efforts, and the efforts of school groups and neighborhood volunteers, is The BirdHouse.

It's technically a project of Dignity of Man, a nonprofit whose mission includes lofty goals, such as, "Making the world a more equitable, sustainable and healthy place for every living thing." For the BirdHouse team, that means starting with growing things. There's an impressive community garden hidden behind two houses that serves as the hub for BirdHouse activities, including classes, workshops, and even a community choir. A variety of fruits, vegetables, herbs, and other plants are thriving here, irrigated by a greywater system, warmed by the California sun, and basking in the glow of the nearby Hollywood Sign. That's only one of the many BirdHouse ecological projects in this Beachwood Canyon neighborhood of Hollywood.

The BirdHouse calendar is filled with ways to engage, donate, and participate in gardening and permaculture, music and other arts, plant medicines, and many other topics and activities. The BirdHouse recognizes that Hollywood is on unceded land of the Tongva people, and that, as guests here, we should recognize the land as sacred, and treat it as such, abolish white supremacy and a hierarchy based on human differences, and learn how to thrive in communities, together.

Address 2460 N Gower Street, Hollywood, CA 90068, www.atthebirdhouse.org | Getting there Bus DASH Beachwood Canyon to Beachwood/Cheremoya | Hours See website for calendar of classes and events | Tip The Garden of Oz is a nearby elaborate tribute to the classic movie *The Wizard of Oz*, lovingly built into a residential yard. Don't go in without permission, but do take a look from the sidewalk (3040 Ledgewood Drive).

8_ The Black Cat

Gay rights born in Hollywood

Hollywood is known these days as a bastion of LGBTQIA+ rights. Many artists in the entertainment industry, both in front of and behind the camera, are members of this community. Plot lines about gay relationships are more abundant than ever before, and more and more people feel comfortable and safe being themselves in and around film and television sets. There's still a lot of room for improvement, but we've come a long way from the days when it was a crime to be gay, and Hollywood attempted to present an all-hetero image.

In 1967, you could be convicted of several anti-gay crimes, such as "lewd conduct," which included kissing. Such a conviction meant not only an arrest, but also that you would have to register as a sex offender. So, when Los Angeles Police officers raided The Black Cat just after midnight on New Year's Eve, when lots of people were, of course, kissing, pandemonium ensued. Many patrons ran and tried to blend in with the crowd at the bar across the street, some fought back, and others were beaten and dragged out of the club and into the street.

Those involved that night couldn't have known the significance the events would have. It was the final straw after eons of persecution. Activists got busy, and in February 1967, a rally outside The Black Cat brought out hundreds of supporters and helped launch the burgeoning gay rights movement. This was two years before the more famous Stonewall uprising in New York, which many people falsely think was the start of the movement. The court case from the raid ultimately failed, but the movement was born.

The Black Cat was designated as an historic site in 2008 for the monumental contribution to LGBTQIA+ rights. Although it has changed hands many times and has had lots of different names, it is once again called The Black Cat. They serve good food and drinks, and kissing on New Year's Eve is encouraged.

Address 3909 W Sunset Boulevard, Hollywood, CA 90029, +1 (323) 661-6369, www.theblackcatla.com | Getting there Bus 2, 4 to Sunset/Hyperion | Hours Mon–Thu 4pm–2am, Fri–Sun 2pm–2am | Tip There are all kinds of great Queer events and performances nearby at Akbar (4356 W Sunset Boulevard, www.akbarsilverlake.com).

9 Buster Keaton's Hollywood

Funny places from classic films

A desperate man comes running out of an alleyway, pursued by dozens of frenzied police officers. He rushes across the street and turns to face the horde. Just before they descend on him, he reaches out with one hand and grabs hold of a car as it zooms by. He is lifted off the ground and yanked away to safety in the nick of time. It's an iconic moment from early cinema.

The scene is from *Cops*, a brilliant silent movie from 1922, and the desperate man is the legendary Buster Keaton. The classic moment, like so many street scenes from Keaton's films, was shot right here in the heart of Hollywood. The alley, on Cahuenga Boulevard just south of Hollywood Boulevard, looks different now, but it's still easy to picture Buster right here, flying sideways as the car whisks him away.

Keaton's studio was nearby at 1021 Lillian Way, so it was logical to make his movies close by. There's a plaque where the studio used to be, rightly commemorating the spot as important to film and Hollywood history. For sticklers, you'll notice that plaque is on the wrong corner – it really ought to be across the street.

At 1622 and 1623 Cahuenga, a discerning Keaton fan may recognize spots from several films, including *The Cameraman*, *Neighbors*, and *Go West*, where Keaton memorably walked his cow down the sidewalk. If you go to the Hollywood La Brea Gateway, you'll be standing in the spot where Keaton opened the safe in *Sherlock, Jr.* and walked right through it onto the street. Looking up Vine Street toward the Hollywood Sign is where we saw an angry mob of jilted brides chasing poor Buster past the DWP power station at 1007 Vine Street to the corner of Eleanor.

For any early film fan, visiting the spots throughout Hollywood where the surprising stunts and hilarious gags from your favorite movies were actually filmed is a wonderful way to remember the enduring legend of Buster Keaton.

Address 1021 Lillian Way, Hollywood, CA 90038 | Getting there Bus 4, 210 to Santa Monica/Vine | Hours Unrestricted | Tip Half a block from the site of Keaton's studio is the Broadwater Theater Complex, home to beloved Los Angeles theater company Sacred Fools (1076 Lillian Way, www.sacredfools.org).

10_ Canterbury Suites

Old Hollywood glamour meets the punks

The way the lyrics begin don't exactly make it sound wonderful, with lines like "whores outside a-posing" and "Fighting off the roaches." But if you listen to the 1979 Go-Go's song *Living at the Canterbury* all the way through, you'll get a more complete picture: "We can do what we want / We can say what we please / We can be who we want / Being poor's okay by me / Living at the Canterbury / My friends think I'm a fool / Living at the Canterbury / I guess it's pretty cool."

It was an electric moment in popular culture. Punk and New Wave music was bursting onto the music scene in New York and London, and in Los Angeles, it was all happening right here in Hollywood, at the rundown building called the Canterbury Suites. There were 50 or so young punks, all living here, dormitory style, and creating the art, fashion, and lifestyle that would soon sweep the globe. It was Hollywood's version of New York's Chelsea Hotel, complete with tragic overdoses, violence, and pain, but with lots of creativity, passion, and joy as well.

The punk rock era isn't the only time the building had famous residents. During Hollywood's Golden Age, Bette Davis and her mother lived here for two years. Giant stars like Bing Crosby, Clara Bow, and Buster Keaton all lived here at various times as well. In the 1980s, it became the home of punk bands, including the Dead Kennedys and of course the Go-Go's, who immortalized the place with their song.

Over the last several years, the Canterbury Suites got rid of all the cockroaches and most of the punk rockers. It was fixed up nicely for a while as a boutique hotel with Parisian-looking red umbrellas and tables out front. Alas, the hotel closed in early 2023, but it's still the same striking 1927 apartment building it's always been. Its colorful history is here to stay, although the next chapter is yet to be written. As the song goes, "I guess it's pretty cool."

Address 1746 Cherokee Avenue, Hollywood, CA 90028 | **Getting there** Bus DASH Hollywood to Whitley/Yucca | **Hours** Lobby unrestricted | **Tip** The building on the southeast corner of Cherokee Avenue and Hollywood Boulevard was the basement home of the legendary punk club The Masque, conveniently located so that residents of the Canterbury could crawl home after a rough night (6646 Hollywood Boulevard).

11__ The Canyon Country Store

Laurel Canyon's rock 'n' roll deli

In the classic Doors song, "Love Street," Jim Morrison writes, "There's a store where the creatures meet." He was talking about the Canyon Country Store. Morrison used to live right across the street and was often part of an impromptu jam session at the store, alongside other legendary musicians like Joni Mitchell, Frank Zappa, and legions of other luminaries, many of whom lived in the canyon nearby.

Laurel Canyon has been a popular place to live for thousands of years. The Tongva people inhabited this area, which had a spring-fed stream and plentiful wildlife. In the beginning of the 20th century, the growing sprawl of Los Angeles took a liking to it as well. When the building that would eventually become the country store was built in 1900, it was called the Bungalow Lodge, used by deer hunters who had to take a "trackless trolley" to get there. The wooden lodge burned down in 1929, and when it was rebuilt with brick this time, it served as a market.

Laurel Canyon became a counterculture hub in the 1960s, and many notable musicians moved there. Neil Young, Linda Ronstadt, James Taylor, and so many others lived here, and the store was a place to meet, eat, and play. By the 1970s, a criminal element had moved into the neighborhood, which was a central clearinghouse for the drug trade. In 1981, four members of the Wonderland Gang, who controlled much of the cocaine trade in LA, were murdered not far from the store.

The neighborhood remains popular, and famous folks still live in these hills. Jennifer Aniston ran the cash register here before her big break on *Friends*. So just imagine that anyone you see here could be the next big star. The Country Store continues to be a delicious deli and market, where you can read old newspaper clippings on the walls and maybe meet some old timers, who were there in the glory days and are happy to tell you all about it.

Address 2108 Laurel Canyon Boulevard, Hollywood, CA 90046, +1 (323) 654-8091, www.facebook.com/CanyonCountryStore | **Getting there** By car, turn north on Laurel Canyon Boulevard from Hollywood Boulevard or W Sunset Boulevard. | **Hours** Tue & Thu 9am–9pm, Wed 9am–10pm, Fri–Mon 9am–11pm | **Tip** You can arrange a private yoga class at Stella Valente's retreat-like studio in Laurel Canyon (www.stellavalente.com/stellayoga).

12 Capitol Records
The music capital of Hollywood

The Capitol Records building is one of the most iconic buildings in Hollywood – or anywhere. It was the world's first circular office building, and there's no other building anywhere that continuously spells out H-O-L-L-Y-W-O-O-D on the rooftop spire in Morse Code. This 13-story tower is also the American record label of the Beatles, who recorded in London but came here often. Their stars on the Walk of Fame, both as a band and as individuals, are right in front of this building.

Constructed in 1956, the Capitol Records building houses four recording studios. The largest, Studio A, is famous for both its sound and its great echo chamber, which was designed by guitar great Les Paul. Located 30 feet underground, the chamber produces reverb that can last for five seconds. Listen to the classic Beach Boys song, *Good Vibrations*, and you'll hear the effect in all of its glory.

The studios are, of course, also known for many legendary artists who have recorded there, from Frank Sinatra to Bob Dylan. Sinatra was the very first artist to record at Capitol, but, oddly, not as a singer. His first session at Capitol was actually as the conductor of an instrumental record called *Frank Sinatra Conducts Tone Poems Of Color*, not exactly his most well-known work. Eventually, of course, he made many famous recordings here. Reportedly, he liked to have sessions that lasted all night long and wanted an audience. So he would invite the secretaries to attend, which most loved to do. To keep them awake long into the night, he'd bring in ice cream.

On the south side of the building's first floor is a mural by artist Richard Wyatt, depicting some of the biggest names in jazz, including Billie Holliday, Charlie Parker, Nat King Cole, and so many more. In 2012, the mural was restored onto ceramic tiles, ensuring that it will last long into the future.

Address 1750 N Vine Street, Hollywood, CA 90028, +1 (323) 871-5001, www.capitolrecords.com | Getting there Metro B to Hollywood/Vine (Red Line); bus 210, 217, 222 to Hollywood/Vine | Hours Unrestricted from outside only | Tip Right down the street is the Pantages Theatre, an art deco masterpiece and one of the premiere places to see live theater (6233 Hollywood Boulevard, www.broadwayinhollywood.com/visit/hollywoodpantagestheatre).

13 __ Charlie Chaplin Studio
Storybook cottages and music legends

Charlie Chaplin made many of his classic films here, including *City Lights*, *Modern Times*, *The Gold Rush*, and more. It's a unique place, designed and built in 1917 to look like a row of English country homes, complete with a Tudor mansion and Colonial cottages. The *Los Angeles Times* called it a "fairy-tale cottage complex." Although it's been through a lot of changes since the silent movie era, it still feels that way today.

Chaplin sold the place in 1957, and in 1966, Herb Albert and Jerry Moss turned it into A&M Records, where hundreds of hit songs were recorded. All four of the Beatles recorded here individually, not to mention Diana Ross, U2, The Rolling Stones, Alicia Keyes, Bruce Springsteen, and so many more. The classic charity song "We Are The World" was recorded here in 1985. It was an unprecedented event in Hollywood, featuring a thrilling group of superstars. The song was written by Michael Jackson and Lionel Ritchie and featured all the biggest recording legends of the day. The Jackson Five, The Pointer Sisters, Ray Charles, Bob Dylan, Tina Turner, and more than 40 other giants of the industry sang the song, which became the fastest selling pop single in American History. Amazingly, 50 more artists wanted to be part of it but had to be turned away because there simply wasn't enough space for them.

Today, the storybook cottages are home to Henson Recording Studios, where the Muppets make their magic. A giant statue of Kermit the Frog dressed as Chaplin's Little Tramp stands at the iconic gates. It's a fitting tribute to the history of these charming studios. The funny but classy brand of humor offered up by the Muppets perfectly encapsulates the legacy the Charlie Chaplin set in motion over a century ago. Kermit is probably a bigger celebrity than Chaplin at this point in history, but both loom large here at the Henson (aka Chaplin) studios.

Address 1416 N La Brea Avenue, Hollywood, CA 90028, www.hensonrecording.com |
Getting there Bus 212 to Sunset/La Brea | **Hours** Unrestricted from outside only |
Tip For a relaxing massage or facial, you're not far from the urban oasis of Blossom Spa
(1350 N Highland Avenue, Unit B, www.blossomspahollywood.com).

14 __ Chase Bank Mosaics

Art is everywhere

The very first full-length film ever made was *The Squaw Man*, filmed right here in Hollywood in 1913. One of the locations where it was shot became the site of a Home Savings of America branch in 1968. Another bank, ho-hum, what's the big deal? The designer of the building was the influential artist Millard Sheets, who was already a nationally known painter in the world of fine art. One of his biggest fans was wealthy financier Howard Ahmanson, and, luckily for art and architecture lovers, Ahmanson didn't care that Sheets wasn't a licensed architect. The painter wound up designing more than 80 branches of Home Savings of America, and this one, in the heart of Hollywood, was reportedly his favorite. It is now a Chase Bank, but its beauty remains intact.

Sheets had an ideology that helped guide his design philosophy: He didn't just want art to be displayed in or on buildings, he also wanted to integrate artwork into the design, which may explain why he had a real passion for tile mosaics. In choosing the subject matter for the mosaics at this branch, Sheets looked to the roots of the location and decided to celebrate the history he found. Consequently, the huge mosaic on the front of the building depicts big Hollywood stars from the Silent Era through 1968, in some of their most memorable roles. Around the back of the bank, the artwork continues. There are stained-glass windows by Susan Hertel, featuring whimsical chase scenes from many movie classics, including *The Squaw Man*.

Today the building is recognized by architecture buffs as a wonderful example of New Formalist design. Of course, it is still a functional place, so by all means, if you need to do some banking, you're welcome to head inside during business hours. But the real joy of this unique bank is found outside, where the marriage of art and architecture is on view at all hours of the day or night.

Address 1500 N Vine Street, Hollywood, CA 90028 | Getting there Metro B to Hollywood/ Vine (Red Line) | Hours Unrestricted | Tip Another architectural wonder is the Cinerama Dome, a former movie theater in a spectacular geodesic dome (6360 Sunset Boulevard, www.laconservancy.org/locations/cinerama-dome).

15 The Chemosphere
Living in the future

Since 1961, there's been a flying saucer nestled in the Hollywood Hills. It's resting on a steep hillside, defying gravity as it extends out over the abyss. It looks as though the spaceship is ready for takeoff once the aliens have finished their invasion. It's not a movie set. But how can such an impossible scene be real?

Welcome to the Chemosphere. In 1960, renowned architect John Lautner was faced with the daunting prospect of building a house on a lot with a nearly 45-degree slope, considered by most to be unbuildable. His solution resulted in Chemosphere, named for the Chem Seal company whose resins were used in construction. This house is both stunning and weird, and it looks like a place where creatures from outer space would feel right at home. The wide, octagonal house stands on a single five-foot-wide pillar, and to make it even stranger, the only way to reach the place is via a funicular. The crazy design has made the house famous.

It is only fitting, therefore, that such an unusual place would have a bizarre story associated with it. What happened is chilling, and it all took place back in 1976. The second owner of the house was a man named Dr. Richard Kuhn, who was a physician working in Southeast Los Angeles. His lover, a 19-year-old named Garland Campbell, broke into the house with another man, Alfred Tolliver, ostensibly to rob the place. Dr. Kuhn was home, and the intruders stabbed him to death during the fracas. Both men were given life sentences.

In 2004, the Chemosphere was recognized as a Los Angeles Historic-Cultural monument, and this is Hollywood, so the house can be seen in movies, of course. It makes an appearance in the 2015 film *Tomorrowland* and 2000's *Charlie's Angels*, but most notably in Brian De Palma's thriller *Body Double,* where you can sense, in every nail-biting frame, the real-life horrors that the house has seen.

Address 7776 Torreyson Drive, Hollywood, CA 90046, www.laconservancy.org/locations/malin-residence-chemosphere | Getting there By car, take Mulholland Drive through the Hollywood Hills, then turn on Torreyson Drive | Hours Unrestricted from outside only | Tip Just a quarter of a mile back down Mulholland is the Universal City Overlook. It's just a turnout on the road, but on a clear day, the vista is amazing (7701 Mulholland Drive, www.mrca.ca.gov/parks/park-listing/universal-city-overlook).

16_Cirque School
For when you're ready to join the circus

Aloysia Gavre was an aerialist with the one and only Cirque du Soleil, performing all over the globe in the early part of this century before she moved to Hollywood. In the circus world, hers was among the topmost jobs. So what does one do after such a career pinnacle? Aloysia badly wanted to train and rehearse with her new ensemble, Troupe Vertigo, who were, pardon the pun, just getting off the ground. They found a huge space in Hollywood that was suitable for the necessary rigging that aerialists and acrobats need. But how could they afford a 6,000-square-foot playground? The answer has deep roots, not only in circus arts, but in all of theater. They would open their space to the public, and the masters would train the next generation of circus performers. Voila! Cirque School was born.

It was 2009 when Aloysia and her partner Rex Camphuis founded what would quickly become revered as the only college of circus arts in Hollywood, and also one of the most respected circus schools anywhere. Totally appropriate for a circus school in Hollywood, the quirky entrance is a dim walk through an alleyway on Hollywood Boulevard. Back when this place was the service shop for the Cadillac dealership that used to be next door, walking down this alley probably wouldn't have been weird at all.

Inside, the space feels like part gym, part theater, part family reunion. The school's motto, "For anybody with any body," accurately sets the tone of an inclusive and caring community, where all are welcome and encouraged to achieve great heights. The school offers a wide range of classes for adults and kids, taught by some of the most accomplished circus artists in the world. They've helped famous people, such as Reese Witherspoon and Christoph Waltz, prepare for roles. And naturally, this is the place where film and television productions go for all manner of circus-related skills and thrills.

Address 5640 1/2 Hollywood Boulevard, Hollywood, CA 90028, +1 (424) 226-2477, www.cirqueschoolla.com, info@cirqueschool.com | Getting there Metro B to Hollywood/ Western (Red Line); bus 180, 207, 217 to Hollywood/Wilton | Hours See website for class schedule, performances, and special events | Tip You're close to Thai Town where there are many great restaurants. Sanamluang is a local favorite (5176 Hollywood Boulevard, www.sanamluanghollywood.com).

17 __ The Comedy Store

Ghosts of Ciro's

The famous Comedy Store in Hollywood used to be a nightclub called Ciro's, an extremely popular nightspot from 1940 to 1957. If you wanted to be seen with A-listers like Frank Sinatra, Marilyn Monroe, Jimmy Stewart, or Marlene Dietrich, Ciro's was your best bet. It was Lana Turner's favorite club too. The list of celebrities who frequented the place was long and illustrious.

Ciro's wasn't only popular with famous faces, though. The club was also the center of organized crime in Los Angeles. Many well-known mobsters hung out there, such as Bugsy Siegel and Johnny Roselli. There were private rooms for gambling and other nefarious activities. And the basement? You really did not want to go down there. Suffice it to say that it was known as the torture room, and very bad things happened there.

When Ciro's closed its doors in 1957, the unspeakable activities in the basement ceased as well. But the Comedy Store is still a place for A-listers. Top comics grace the stage here nightly. The only kind of torture you're likely to encounter these days is a comedian having an off night. But echoes of that painful past remain. After the club became the Comedy Store in 1978, people began to report paranormal activity there, with reports of chairs moving by themselves, coins falling from the ceiling, and other unexplainable phenomena. Those who are brave enough to venture into the basement have reported spirits and heard sounds of distress – perhaps some unlucky ghosts who tangled with the Mob?

One ghost who has been spotted on multiple occasions is that of comic Steve Lubetkin, a regular at the club. He seemingly blamed his suicide in 1979 on the club's owner, who had not given him any performance slots after a pay strike. He leapt off the hotel next to the club. The note found in his pocket read. "My name is Steve Lubetkin. I used to work at the Comedy Store."

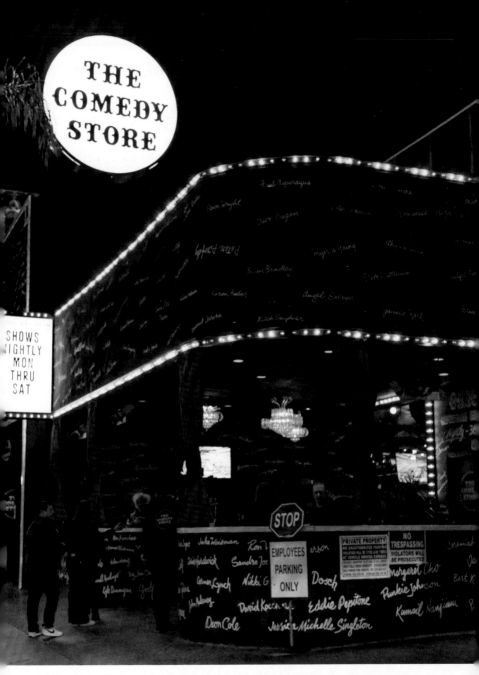

Address 8433 W Sunset Boulevard, Hollywood, CA 90069, +1 (323) 650-6268,
www.thecomedystore.com | Getting there Bus 2 to Sunset/Kings | Hours Daily 7pm–2am |
Tip The Laugh Factory, another one of the top comedy venues in the country, is down the
street (8001 W Sunset Boulevard, www.laughfactory.com).

18 __ Crossroads of the World

The country's first outdoor shopping mall

The details of Charles Crawford's murder are somewhat murky. It was 1931, and Crawford's empire of brothels and casinos in Los Angeles was crumbling. He had thrived during the Roaring Twenties, but he now faced multiple charges. One night in May, he and his associate Herbert Spencer met at their office with former deputy district attorney David Clark, who was running to be a judge in Los Angeles. Clark claims that Crawford tried to talk him into a scheme to frame the chief of police and that Crawford pulled a gun when Clark refused to go along. The truth of what happened will never be known, but what is certain is that Crawford and Spencer were both dead at the end of the night.

Crawford's widow Ella wanted to do something special with the land where her husband had been murdered, and the idea of Crossroads of the World was born. She imagined a place where people could buy merchandise from around the globe. Designer Robert V. Derrah ran with the concept. Built in 1936 to resemble an ocean liner, the shopping center is considered the first outdoor mall. It originally held 57 shops and cafés, each designed to represent the wares of a single country. There was a restaurant called A Bit of Italy, a barbershop named The Barber of Seville, and dozens more. The ship sailed down the center of the mall, and The Continental Café on the 2nd floor provided a place for guests to dine "on the upper deck."

In the 1950s, the venue was converted into an office complex but maintained its distinct maritime spirit. Many luminaries of movies and music had their offices here, including Alfred Hitchcock, F. Scott Fitzgerald, Jackson Browne, and others.

It's been the site of lots of shooting over the years, but fortunately not the kind that cost Charles Crawford his life. Many films and TV shows have been shot here, including *L.A. Confidential*, *Indecent Proposal*, and *Dragnet*.

Address 6671 W Sunset Boulevard, Hollywood, CA 90028, www.crossroadsoftheworldla.com | Getting there Metro B to Hollywood/Highland (Red Line); bus 2 to Sunset/Cherokee | Hours Unrestricted from outside only | Tip Less than a block away is the Catalina Jazz Club, where jazz greats have always played (6725 W Sunset Boulevard, www.catalinajazzclub.com).

19 El Capitan Theatre
The amazing premiere of Citizen Kane

Developer Charles E. Toberman, known as "the father of Holly-wood," wanted the El Capitan Theatre to dazzle audiences when they arrived to see a play. So he called on Morgan, Walls & Clements, renowned architects who had designed many landmark buildings in Los Angeles, to craft a stunner in the Spanish Baroque style. They teamed with G. Albert Lansburgh, who filled the elaborate interior with ornate details that remain breathtaking to all who visit.

The building, completed in 1926, was the toast of the town for years, with successful runs of some of the biggest plays of the era. And then, in 1941, something extraordinary occurred. The drama that happened behind the scenes turned this playhouse into a proper Hollywood movie palace.

In early 1941, a filmmaker named Orson Welles, barely 26 years old, had completed the now classic film *Citizen Kane*. But there was a problem. He couldn't find a theater willing to take the risk of showing it. Most critics who attended pre-screenings of the film raved, but one called it "a vicious attack" on newspaper magnate William Randolph Hearst. That's all it took to create a firestorm. Hearst refused to let any of his papers write about the film and even tried to buy it outright so he could destroy the negative. Lawsuits were threatened and filed, and Radio City Music Hall, where the premiere had been scheduled, was pressured into canceling the screening. Welles scrambled to find a the-ater to show his film, and on May 8, 1941, the El Capitan rose to the occasion. The theater has shown first-run movies ever since.

Nowadays, the fully restored El Capitan is owned by Disney, who have put considerable resources into restoring it to its full glory. This is where premieres of Disney features take place, with all of the beauty and fanfare, but none of the worry and drama of the famous premiere that changed the theater's destiny.

Address 6838 Hollywood Boulevard, Hollywood, CA 90028, +1 (323) 491-1500, elcapitantheatre.com | **Getting there** Metro B to Hollywood/Highland (Red Line); bus 212, 217 to Hollywood/Highland | **Hours** See website for schedule | **Tip** Also on this strip of Hollywood Boulevard is the newly restored, gorgeous Egyptian Theater, built in 1922 and well worth a look (6712 Hollywood Boulevard, www.americancinematheque.com/about/theatres/egyptian-theatre).

20__El Cid

Old-world entertainment

Hollywood is the hub of entertainment, so it should come as no surprise that even some of the restaurants have a sense of whimsy and fun. There have been many themed eateries over the years, including the Pirate's Den, where patrons could be kidnapped by a band of unruly scallywags, and Saddle Ranch, where you can roast your own marshmallows over a fire after riding a mechanical bull. But there's no place like El Cid.

Founded by flamenco dancers Juan Talavera and Margarita Cordova, El Cid is the only club in Hollywood designed to feel like a 16th-century Spanish tavern. The paella and tapas are wonderful, and you can enjoy a full four-course Spanish meal, while watching a Flamenco show, still running regularly after more than fifty years.

There's a history of whimsical design in this building, one of the oldest in Hollywood. Before it became El Cid in 1962, it was the Cabaret Concert Theatre, a favorite of many of Hollywood's elite. Before that, it was the Gateway Theatre. From 1925 to 1932, when the country was in the throes of prohibition, but illicit booze flowed in Hollywood, folks had a grand old time on a night out by going to jail – Jail Café, that is.

The Jail Café, complete with stone walls and a guard tower on top, was all the rage. Patrons dined behind bars, while waiters dressed as guards or prisoners served them. Yes, it's problematic to have an all-white clientele (which it was) having fun pretending to be locked up like the mostly black (which it still is) prison population, but a century ago, such awareness was yet to come to Hollywood, and the Jail Café didn't pretend to be politically correct.

An evening at El Cid has no such issues. Sip sangria on one of the outdoor patios, or enjoy a performance, from flamenco, to rock, to burlesque, and let your mind drift to old world Spain, without the risk of being kidnapped or locked up by the charming waitstaff.

Address 4212 Sunset Boulevard, Hollywood, CA 90026, +1 (323) 668-0318, www.elcidsunset.com | Getting there Bus 2 to Sunset/Bates | Hours Tue–Sun 5–11pm, see website for performance schedule | Tip Just down Sunset is snooty coffee lovers' heaven, Intelligentsia. Pricey but worth it (3922 Sunset Boulevard, www.intelligentsia.com).

21 El Coyote

Best place for your last margarita

On August 8, 1969, actress Sharon Tate and her ex-boyfriend Jay Sebring, along with two of their friends, went to this legendary Mexican restaurant for dinner. They would have pulled up under the red-and-white cursive of the iconic sign and walked into the kitschy and cool spot that still looks largely the same today as it did then. Colorful décor, hundreds of Mexican tchotchkes, and ubiquitous Christmas lights embellish every corner of all five rooms in the large restaurant.

They sat at the bar while they waited for their table, where they likely chatted with some of the personable staff, many of whom have worked there for decades. Sharon reportedly ordered enchiladas, which, like everything on the menu at El Coyote, was probably delicious. Being eight and a half months pregnant, she hopefully skipped the margarita, a staple here, which is served in an ambitious glass that requires some revelers to use both hands to heave the boozy tub up to their mouths.

It's safe to assume that the meal was a delight, which has been true for most patrons ever since El Coyote first opened in 1931. After eating, the four of them drove back to Sharon's house in Benedict Canyon, where she lived with her husband, film director Roman Polanski, who was out of town. Later that night, along with another one of their friends, the four were brutally murdered by members of the Manson Family.

News of the awful killings stunned the world, and some say that it darkened the whole tone of the country and abruptly "ended the Sixties." The stain of the tragedy still resonates throughout Hollywood and beyond, but El Coyote remains a place for great food and amazing margaritas. You can dine in the same red leather booth where Sharon and her friends ate that night, and despite the macabre history, statistics show that almost everyone survives well beyond their tasty meals.

Address 7312 Beverly Boulevard, Hollywood, CA 90036, +1 (323) 939-2255, www.elcoyotecafe.com | **Getting there** By car, drive south on La Brea Avenue to Beverly Boulevard and turn right | **Hours** Sun, Wed & Thu noon–9pm, Fri & Sat noon–10pm | **Tip** Pan Pacific Park, two blocks to the West, has a poignant Holocaust Memorial that is largely unknown (7600 Beverly Boulevard, www.laparks.org/reccenter/pan-pacific).

22 — Escape Hotel Hollywood
Horror-filled entertainment and fine dining

It's easy to check into this hotel, but getting out is not guaranteed. This house of horrors is an entire 1930s-styled hotel, in which every room is a different and terrifying escape game that will make you feel like you're in a vintage horror film. The themed rooms include Slaughterhouse, Zombie, and Circus, and they are each filled with scary puzzles and mysteries that you and your friends have to solve in an hour if you want to get out alive. For fans of the horror and mystery genres who enjoy putting themselves in the perilous story, these escape rooms are a thrill and a delight. This is actually the world's largest escape room complex, and it's popular with all sorts of people, including many celebrities. Angelina Jolie has been spotted here with her kids, and Tom Holland and Will Smith once attempted an escape here together.

Room Number 13 at the Escape Hotel is its own wonderful experience. Not an escape room at all, Room Number 13 is a cocktail lounge and restaurant that whisks you back in time to the golden age of Hollywood. The art deco décor and beautiful design is a perfect setting for the exquisite show and provocative mood they're stirring up here. Be sure to book a reservation on a Saturday night, when there's an entertaining floor show in the style of a 1930s cabaret with a sexy flair.

Getting into Room 13 requires that you locate the secret staircase and ascend to the balcony level overlooking the stunning lobby, where nervous patrons are checking in and eagerly anticipating their escape room experiences. You're likely to see some of the spooky characters from the hotel wandering around the lounge and restaurant, which only adds to the ambiance.

Are you daring enough to check into the escape hotel? If you're not, it's understandable. Just choose Room 13 and enjoy a drink while the daredevils risk it all in the unknown horrors of the hotel.

Address 6633 Hollywood Boulevard, Hollywood, CA 90028, +1 (323) 848-4954, www.escapehotelhollywood.com, room13@escapehotelhollywood.com | Getting there Bus 217 to Hollywood/Las Palmas | Hours See website for hours | Tip Go on the two-hour Haunted Hollywood Tour if you love spooky stuff, starting in front of the Pantages Theater, and take a peek into the murky gloom of dark Hollywood legends (6233 Hollywood Boulevard, www.viator.com/tours).

23   Famous Amos Square
A Black entrepreneur and a delicious cookie

The Bossa Nova restaurant is a delightful place, where visitors will be rewarded with an exquisite Brazilian meal and a possible celebrity sighting, as this is a favorite eatery for many stars. But this is also the location of the original Famous Amos Cookie Shop, which is why the plaque on this Hollywood street corner calls it Famous Amos Square.

Wallace Amos, Jr. was already very accomplished when he started his cookie company. He was the first Black agent at the William Morris talent agency (or any other agency for that matter), where he worked with many legends, signing Simon and Garfunkel and Marvin Gaye, among many others. But when his career as an agent began to falter, Amos turned to something that had filled him with joy as a child: baking cookies the way his Aunt Della had taught him.

The cookies were delicious, and he baked them obsessively. He became known as "the agent with the cookies" and would show up to every meeting with a freshly baked bag of chocolate chip perfection. Some might say that such a delicious tactic would make anyone the most successful agent ever, but it wasn't so in Amos' case. His career continued to decline, and so he decided to make baking a full-time pursuit.

The treats were wonderful, and everyone seemed to love them. But he needed some seed money to start his business. Amos still had a lot of friends and associates in the music business, so he turned to his rolodex for investors. Marvin Gaye and Helen Reddy threw in the initial investment for Amos to secure the cookie venue, and the rest is crispy, chocolatey, yummy history.

Famous Amos became one of the most recognizable cookie brands internationally, with Amos himself as the warm and gregarious pitchman. The company was eventually bought up by a major food conglomerate. But this little unassuming street corner in Hollywood was where the delectable story began.

Address 7181 Sunset Boulevard, Hollywood, CA 90046 | Getting there Bus 2 to Sunset/ La Brea | Hours Unrestricted | Tip Plummer Park has a delightful little farmer's market on Monday mornings (7377 Santa Monica Boulevard).

24_ Ferndell Murder
Nature "museum" with a secret

Jean Elizabeth Spangler's purse was discovered near the entrance to Ferndell two days after she disappeared in October 1949. Over 150 police officers and volunteers combed the park for more clues, but none were ever found. All these decades later, the mysterious case is still unsolved.

She left behind many questions, but very few answers. Jean had had a long and painful custody dispute with her ex-husband and had gone to talk with him about a child support payment. Was he responsible for her disappearance? Jean had been a dancer at the Florentine Gardens nightclub, where she had reportedly met some mobsters. One of the men she'd been hanging around with, Davy Ogul, was an associate of the infamous Mickey Cohen, and Ogul disappeared two days after Jean did. Were they fleeing from the mob together?

The straps of her handbag were torn, suggesting violence. But perhaps the strangest and most tantalizing clue was found inside. She had written a cryptic note to someone named Kirk: "...Can't wait any longer, Going to see Dr. Scott. It will work best this way..." Jean was, in fact, three months pregnant, and movie star Kirk Douglas admitted that she had recently been cast in a small role in his latest film. He said that he'd been "kidding around" with her on the set. Was he the "Kirk" from the note? Was Jean going to get a (then illegal) abortion? We may never know.

The beautiful and shadowy Ferndell "nature museum" (as lovingly designated by the city), with all of its pathways, bridges, trails, and waterfalls, still hasn't given up its secret. But the waters here are said to possess mystical powers. It's a stunning walk along a spring-fed stream filled with tropical greenery and cool shade even in the heat of summer. So enjoy the half-mile stroll through the open-air "museum," but keep your eyes peeled for any clues that the years may have concealed.

Address Fern Dell Drive, Hollywood, CA 90027, +1 (323) 666-5046, www.hikespeak.com/trails/ferndell-trail-griffith-park-western-canyon | **Getting there** By car, turn onto Fern Dell Drive from Los Feliz Boulevard, just east of Western Avenue | **Hours** Daily 6am–10pm | **Tip** There's a very sweet statue of a bear cub at the entrance to Griffith Park (corner of Fern Dell Drive and Los Feliz Boulevard). Watch for it while you drive by, or hop out of the car for a memorable selfie.

25 — Florentine Gardens

Nightclub where Marilyn had her wedding reception

Late in 1941, while World War II raged across the ocean, a strikingly beautiful, 15-year-old foster kid was at a club in Hollywood called The Florentine Gardens. Her name was Norma Jean Baker, and she seemed to be an ordinary high schooler. Perhaps she was there to enjoy the delicious Italian food that they served back then, or to take in a racy burlesque show. Maybe she was there to hear some popular music and to dance on what was touted as "the largest and finest spring dance floor on the Pacific Coast." Whatever the reason, she met a cute older boy there named Jim Dougherty.

It all sounds so romantic. But in reality, the relationship had more to do with the regulations of the foster care system than it did with young love. Jim was the neighbor of Norma Jean's legal guardians, and when they decided to leave the state, Norma Jean knew that she didn't want to go back to the orphanage or move to a new foster family. Instead, on June 19, 1942, only 18 days after her 16th birthday, Jim and Norma Jean were married and held their wedding reception at the club where they first met.

What happened next is well known around the world. After Jim was drafted and went overseas, Norma Jean became a model, changed her name to Marilyn Monroe, and simply put, became an icon of pop culture and one of the most legendary names in Hollywood history.

The venue itself changed names too for a while. It was called The Cotton Club in the 1950s through the 1970s. Since then, it's been a strip club, a Salvation Army post, a school of dentistry, and a salsa club, then back to The Florentine Gardens in 1981. Now, it's mostly rented out for parties and film shoots, but on Sunday nights it's still a nightclub. It's easy to imagine young Norma Jean and Jim cutting a rug on the fancy dance floor, with fame, chaos, and tragedy all still looming in the cloudy future.

Address 5951 Hollywood Boulevard, Hollywood, CA 90028, +1 (562) 286-4209,
www.florentinegardensla.com | **Getting there** Metro B to Hollywood/Vine (Red Line);
bus 180, 217 to Hollywood/Bronson | **Hours** Sun 9pm–2am | **Tip** Just on the other side
of the freeway is the *Hollywood's Village* mural by Juan Pablo Reyes, a tribute to "everything
Hollywood" (S Yucca Street at the 101 Freeway, www.hollywoodvillagemural.org).

26 The Formosa Café
Oldest surviving Red Car

Old timers still get a gleam in their eye when they wax nostalgic about the Los Angeles streetcar system, whose heyday was in the first half of the last century. And why not? The Pacific Electric Railway Company's Red Car system (and the Yellow Car too) was once the largest public transit system in the world, with several stops going right through the heart of Hollywood.

Everyone loved the Red Car. Postcards, advertising, and folklore abounded, and streetcars were featured in many Hollywood movies. In 1925, a prize fighter named Jimmy Bernstein had the brilliant idea to open the Formosa Café in one of the decommissioned trolleys.

So what happened? Why did the golden age of streetcars end? Did the automobile industry titans conspire to crush the Red Car? They certainly had the most to gain from the takeover of the railway by car culture. We may never know the truth about why it failed, but one thing is certain. After the 1920s, the streetcar system began to falter, and over the next couple of decades, it fell into serious disuse and disrepair. The last Red Car line closed in 1961, ending the glory days of Los Angeles streetcars for good.

The Formosa Café remains, however, and it's still one of the best Chinese restaurants in Hollywood. This place used to be a favorite watering hole of Frank Sinatra, Humphrey Bogart, Elvis Presley, and many other stars. The café has gone through renovations over the years, but has been lovingly restored and now features the oldest Red Car still in existence – it's from 1906! A new area of the Formosa is called the Yee Mee Loo Bar, where the décor features stories of early Chinese and Chinese American influence in Hollywood. It's still a favorite place for many Hollywood celebrities, and it's one of the only spots in town to sit in an original Red Car and hear stories of the best streetcars in Hollywood, and the world beyond.

Address 7156 Santa Monica Boulevard, West Hollywood, CA 90046, +1 (323) 850-1014, www.theformosacafe.com, formosa@1933group.com | Getting there Bus 4 to Santa Monica/ Formosa | Hours Mon–Fri 11am–4pm, 5pm–midnight, Sat & Sun 11am–4pm, 5pm–2am | Tip Carney's Deli is another restaurant in a train car in Hollywood, and the food is great too (8351 Sunset Boulevard, www.carneytrain.com).

27_Frances Goldwyn Library

Modern cathedral of books

In 1907, a permanent home for the Hollywood Public Library was built. The idea had been championed by the Women's Club of Hollywood, which garnered the support of Andrew Carnegie to back the ambitious project. It was an immediate success and thrived for decades. By 1923, the library had outgrown the building and moved into a larger space at the current location, where everything was fine and dandy – for a while.

Disaster struck in 1982. An arsonist set fire to the library, and the building, along with most of the 90,000-plus volumes in the collection at that time, was destroyed. The crime was never solved, but local businesses and neighbors weren't going to let the catastrophe spell the end of their library. Various library associations and corporations rallied. People from all around the community chipped in with their own books, and the current, spectacular library opened in 1986, complete with a ribbon-cutting ceremony that featured movie star Kirk Douglas.

Designed by the incomparable Frank Gehry and funded by the Samuel Goldwyn Foundation, the Hollywood Library is a stunning place. Far from the stereotypical dark and musty book vault that some associate with a library experience, the Frances Howard Goldwyn Library, named for the actress and book lover who was married to Samuel Goldwyn, is filled with light that streams in through a five-story window. There's a beautiful circular stairway inside, and there are reflecting pools outside the second floor reading rooms. Say what you will about modern architecture, but this is Gehry, and it definitely has an exciting and breezy vibe.

Consider the location, and you'll understand why this library boasts an impressive collection of books, films, and other media connected to the motion picture industry. It's a great place to learn the history of Hollywood or just to gaze out the massive windows at the city beyond.

Address 1623 Ivar Avenue, Hollywood, CA 90028, +1 (323) 856-8260, www.lapl.org/branches/hollywood | **Getting there** Metro B to Hollywood/Vine (Red Line); bus 217 to Hollywood/Ivar | **Hours** Mon–Thu 10am–8pm, Fri & Sat 9:30am–5:30pm, Sun 1–5pm | **Tip** The storied Ivar Theater right next door is now part of the Los Angeles Film School. Take a tour through the school or attend one of their performances (1605 Ivar Avenue, www.lafilm.edu).

28 The Frolic Room

Dive bar of the stars

Back in 1930, when the country was dry as a bone and the simple act of getting an alcoholic beverage required covert criminal activity, the Frolic Room was born as a speakeasy. It became a legal bar in 1934, after prohibition ended, but the somewhat illicit feeling has never faded. There's a wonderful, dive bar sort of charm to it, too. You get the sense here that you're actually in an authentic bit of Old Hollywood, complete with the classic and delicious cocktails and the glamour – the bartenders actually wear suits and ties. But there's the dark underbelly here as well. Maybe that slightly seedy vibe is what led Charles Bukowski and so many other celebrities to spend so much time here.

In Hollywood's heyday, the annual Oscar awards used to be broadcast from right next door at the historic Pantages Theatre on Hollywood Boulevard. It was a tradition of many stars of that time, including Frank Sinatra, Judy Garland, and so many more, to duck out of the overly long ceremony to grab a beverage at the whimsical-sounding Frolic room, which served as the theater's hospitality center. It was, and still is, a genuine celebrity hangout, and it's very easy to imagine your favorite stars wetting their whistles here.

But don't let the name fool you. This dive-y joint isn't all fun and games. It's also infamous for at least two unsolved murders. It's the last place that Elizabeth Short, aka the Black Dahlia, was seen in 1947 before her mutilated body was found, and in 2010, the doorman of the Frolic Room was murdered here, allegedly by a drunk patron who was never apprehended.

So it's no surprise that the bar was chosen as a location for the iconic noir film *L.A. Confidential,* and so many other movies with dark and mysterious stories. Some may claim they know the truth, but for now, the Frolic Room continues to keep its secrets, like the speakeasy it once was.

Address 6245 Hollywood Boulevard, Hollywood, CA 90028, +1 (323) 462-5890, www.frolicroomla.com | Getting there Metro to Hollywood/Vine (Red Line); bus 180, 217 to Hollywood/Argyle | Hours Daily 11–2am | Tip Stay in gritty mode and visit the Scum and Villainy Cantina, just down the block. The crazy colors of the cocktails aren't the only similarities to the cantina in Star Wars (6377 Hollywood Boulevard, www.scumandvillainycantina.com).

29__Full-Service Body Shop
Secret gay brothel in a gas station

Where the modern fire station stands today at the corner of Holly-wood and Van Ness, there used to be a very special Richfield Oil "service station." Like other gas stations in the 1940s, it offered service and fuel for automobiles. But unlike the average gas station, Scotty Bowers' business offered a whole lot more than a standard oil change. Being gay was illegal, and if you were famous, it was doubly dangerous as both a crime and as a potential career killer.

Scotty employed both male and female sex workers at the gas station. He acted as a "male madam," helping many famous clients, including Rock Hudson, Cole Porter, and the Duke and Duchess of Windsor, enjoy the kind of sex that they desired, sometimes in a safe, convenient trailer behind the station.

Reportedly, two of his most well-known customers were superstars Spencer Tracy and Kathryn Hepburn. They were one of the hottest onscreen couples of their time, playing opposite one another in nine films, and they were also purported to have had an offscreen affair that spanned decades, keeping all the tabloids aflutter. All of that may be racy and perhaps true, but it's even more exciting to think about where they got their (ahem) tires rotated.

According to many sources, including a 2017 documentary about Bowers, he was one of Tracy's lovers himself, and he often set Tracy up with other men at the station and elsewhere. And Kathryn Hepburn? She apparently used Bowers' services to arrange dates with women well over 100 times.

We've come a long way since then, thankfully. Many members of the LGBTQIA+ community are out now and don't need a Scotty Bowers to negotiate their love lives. But standing in front of this fire station today still harkens back to a Hollywood where secret romance was in the air, gas was cheap, and an attractive young attendant was waiting to fill your tank.

Address 5769 Hollywood Boulevard, Hollywood, CA 90028, +1 (213) 485-6282 | Getting there Metro B to Hollywood/Western (Red Line); bus 180, 207, 217 to Hollywood/Wilton | Tip Aspiring acrobats can take an aerial or pole dancing class at Aeriform Arts (1276 N Van Ness Avenue, www.aeriformarts.com).

30 __ Funko Hollywood

Pop yourself!

Whether you're a kid or just a child at heart, the most amazing object that you didn't know you needed is now available in Hollywood. It's a miniature vinyl statue of yourself or a loved one, with an enormous head, huge eyes, and bursting with that peculiar kind of cuteness that exudes from every Funko Pop! figure. You can't order these one-of-a-kind collectibles on the internet, which explains why the Funko Hollywood store consistently has long lines spilling out of the doorway and down Hollywood Boulevard.

The phenomenon of Funko's Pop! figures is well known to those who like to collect memorabilia from their favorite comics, TV shows, and movies. There are thousands of different characters in Funko Pop! form, and more are released all the time. These incredibly popular plastic statues are all over the place – in toy stores, book shops and comic bookstores. Even some clothing stores sell them. But the personalized, "Pop People" experience, where you can customize and create your very own Pop! is only available at the Pop Factory itself, right here in the heart of Hollywood.

Depending on the day and time, you may need to be pretty patient. It can take as long as three hours to complete the popping process during the busiest times, but legions of happy fans say that it's worth the wait. You can't make a reservation, but just know that the early birds get the Funko Pops. There are a limited number made per day, and sometimes the list fills up by 3pm.

After your name is added to the list, you'll have a bit of time to explore the 40,000-square-foot Funko store, which is filled with more than just Pop! figures. There are selfie opportunities galore, with larger-than-life-sized figures everywhere, as well as all kinds of merch, clothing, and fun surprises hidden all around the store, waiting for you to take them home.

Address 6201 Hollywood Boulevard, Hollywood, CA 90028, +1 (213) 462-3600, www.funko.com |
Getting there Metro B to Hollywood/Vine (Red Line); bus 217 to Hollywood/Argyle | Hours
Mon–Fri noon–6pm, Sat & Sun 10–6pm | Tip Afters Ice Cream is a great place to go after,
well, anything. Or before. It's just great, any time (6201 Hollywood Boulevard, Unit 124,
www.aftersicecream.com).

31 Genghis Cohen

Chinese food and music

The name of the restaurant Genghis Cohen is a mash-up of the name of a Mongolian Emperor and a common Jewish surname, but there isn't anything particularly Jewish or Mongolian about the place – unless you think that simply being a wonderful New York-style Chinese restaurant in a pretty Jewish neighborhood qualifies it to be sort of Jewish. After all, they don't use dairy in any of their meat dishes, so it's kind of kosher-ish. They're open on Christmas, making that day not only the toughest reservation in town, but also sort of a Jewish tradition for some. Add to that the fact that the name and place are kind of funny and cool… But actually no. It's still not particularly Mongolian or Jewish. But it absolutely is a great place for seriously good food, drink, and music.

In the last few decades, Genghis Cohen has become something of a Hollywood institution. Since 1983, when original owner Allan Rinde bought and refurbished the run-down pizza joint across the street from where he worked as a music producer, the establishment has been serving wonderful meals and great cocktails, and some call it the best Chinese restaurant in Los Angeles. That's debatable perhaps, but there's a real scene that has grown here too that is undeniable. The attached music venue is small, only 50 seats, but it has seen a stream of wonderful acts over the years, giving it a reputation as a top-level venue. Big names like Joni Mitchell, Stevie Wonder, and Jackson Browne have graced the tiny stage here, as well as countless others, many of whom have gone on to fame.

The Foo Foo Drink menu features whimsical takes on classic cocktails, giving them an Asian, Jewish, American Chinese, or New York-y flair. The drinks will be flowing all night while you enjoy a delicious meal and then sit in the attached music venue to enjoy a set from some fabulous act that might be the next big thing.

Address 740 N Fairfax Avenue, Hollywood, CA 90046, +1 (323) 653-0640, www.genghiscohen.com | Getting there Bus 10, 217, 218 to Melrose/Fairfax | Hours Sun–Thu noon–10pm, Fri & Sat noon–11pm | Tip Cat lovers will want to make a reservation at Hollywood's only cat café, Crumbs and Whiskers, where you can cuddle and adopt a kitten (7924 Melrose Avenue, www.crumbsandwhiskers.com).

32 Goody Store

Treasure hunt in Hollywood

In a neighborhood known as Little Armenia on a gritty part of Santa Monica Boulevard, there's a storefront that's easy to miss. It's slightly rundown, and it's right next to the noisy freeway, with minimal parking. Some folks may not have the constitution to stick it out, but intrepid treasure hunters won't be deterred by these insignificant challenges because inside this tiny, overstuffed shop is an amazing trove of great items for sale, including furniture, electronics, and other gear, at lower prices than Goodwill. It's no surprise that those in the know consider the Goody Store one of the best places in town to go thrifting.

The experience is more than shopping. Rifling through the store is equal parts scavenger hunt and archeological dig. There are so many great items from clothing, to appliances, to toys. Keep an open mind. You might come in hoping for a desk and a toaster and leave with a bed frame, a new pair of jeans, and a cool jar of beads. Most shoppers leave with a full bag and a smile on their face.

The shop is run by the wonderful Rosa, who always goes out of her way to give good prices. She's a big part of why so many people love this store so much. Satisfied shoppers say Rosa will throw in free batteries, add an item or two to their order, or just offer a lower price without even being prompted.

There are good reasons that she's so great at what she does. Rosa has been running this fantastic little store for nearly three decades, and she has definitely gotten the hang of it. Where she finds all of her amazing stuff remains a mystery, but a lot of it seems to be in fantastic condition, or even brand new. Obviously, there's no guarantee that any single visit to the Goody Store will yield the bounty that you were hoping for. But it'll definitely be a fun adventure to try your luck. And Rosa will be here next time you decide to try again.

Address 5421 Santa Monica Boulevard, Hollywood, CA 90029, +1 (323) 363-2456 |
Getting there Bus 4 to Santa Monica/Western | Hours Mon–Sat noon–7pm |
Tip Iguana Vintage Clothing has a massive selection of items you never knew you
needed (6320 Hollywood Boulevard, www.iguanaclothing.com).

33 Griffith Park Observatory
Things are looking up

Since 1935, visitors to the amazing Griffith Observatory have been greeted in the entryway by an enormous Foucault pendulum, a swinging device designed to illustrate the Earth's rotation. After being mesmerized by the dizzying spectacle of the pendulum, you'll be drawn by a loud buzzing to a huge Tesla coil sparking giant bolts of electricity inside its alcove. Although the scientists here assure us that it's safe, it's pretty unnerving.

But if cool science stuff isn't your thing, the observatory is also the location for scores of films and TV shows. In the classic 1955 film *Rebel Without a Cause*, James Dean's character gets into a knife fight in the parking lot, and fans of Dean often come here to take selfies next to the statue of him that looks out at the Hollywood Sign.

Like the park itself, the observatory is named for the wealthy and bizarre Griffith J. Griffith, who claimed to see ghosts in the park and refused to spend the night there. Griffith was tormented by strange notions, including his belief that the pope was conspiring with Griffith's own wife to poison him and steal his money. This wacky idea led him to shoot his wife in the face, an attack that she miraculously survived by leaping out of a window! He wound up spending a couple of years in prison for attempting to murder her, and he lived the rest of his life with that shame surrounding him.

These days, most people don't remember that awful story and simply see Griffith as the oddball philanthropist who gave the park and the observatory to the city. So when visitors to Hollywood are hoping for a star sighting, they happily head up the hill to the Griffith Observatory, which is the only place in town that guarantees it. Millions of curious skygazers have looked through the telescope here, literally the largest number of people ever to have viewed through a single telescope anywhere in the world.

Address 2800 E Observatory Road, Hollywood, CA 90027, +1 (213) 473-0800, www.griffithobservatory.org | Getting there Bus DASH Observatory Shuttle to Griffith Observatory | Hours Tue–Fri noon–10pm, Sat & Sun 10am–10pm | Tip The Greek Theatre just down the hill is one of the best places in the world to see a concert (2700 N Vermont Avenue, www.lagreektheatre.com).

34 __ The H

A sign of hard times

"I am afraid, I am a coward. I am sorry for everything. If I had done this a long time ago, it would have saved a lot of pain. P.F." This reads the devastating note that was found near the body of 24-year-old actress Peg Entwhistle, who leapt to her death from the H of the Hollywood Sign on September 16, 1932. While she's not the only aspiring actress whose Tinseltown dreams ended in tragedy, her story has become a legend, and once you know it, you may never see the sign the same way again.

At the time of Peg's tragic leap, the 50-foot-tall wooden sign spelled out, "Hollywoodland." Four thousand light bulbs flashed in sequence, "HOLLY," "WOOD," and "LAND." It had been installed in 1923 as a temporary advertisement for a new housing development but became so beloved that by the time Peg climbed up a workman's ladder and took her last look out over the city, the sign was already iconic.

Peg lived in the neighborhood below the swanky new houses, on a street where she could see the sign flashing away nightly, and it's easy to imagine how the glamorous blinking monstrosity just mocked her curdled dream of stardom. We don't know all the reasons she made her way up to the top of Mount Lee to ascend the sign, but Peg has come to represent the hard reality that talent and beauty aren't the only ingredients to make fantasies of fame and fortune come true.

The "LAND" was removed in 1949, and the remaining sign fell into disrepair over the subsequent decades. It was restored in 1978, thanks to a small handful of donors, including celebrities like Hugh Hefner, Gene Kelly, and Alice Cooper. These days, there are no flashing lights, but the sign itself is a kind of shining beacon representing the glitz and allure of the movie business, as well as the haunting memory of Peg, and so many other souls lost to the empty promise of the Hollywood dream.

Address Top of Mount Lee in Griffith Park, +1 (213) 300-0108, www.hollywoodsign.org |
Getting there Bus DASH Observatory Shuttle to Griffith Observatory, hike from Bronson
Canyon or Griffith Observatory | Hours Daily dawn–dusk | Tip On the north side
of Griffith Park is Forest Lawn Cemetery, where you can visit the graves of Buster Keaton,
Stan Laurel, and many other celebrities (6300 Forest Lawn Drive, www.forestlawn.com).

35 The High Tower

The pointless siege of Fort Anthony

Not far from the Hollywood Bowl is a five-story structure resembling an Italian bell tower. It's actually an elevator built around 1920, and if you're lucky enough to live in one of the storied homes perched up on the hillside, this lift is how you get to your front door. Elegant, stately, and five stories tall, the High Tower has been in many movies for obvious reasons. The 1935 duplex built by architect Carl Kay adjacent to the tower was Phillip Marlowe's apartment in the classic Robert Altman film *The Long Goodbye*. Only residents have a key to ride the elevator, but hiking the stairways in this historic neighborhood is well worth the sweaty effort.

But there's a dark history to this quiet cluster of homes. So after you've admired the tower, keep walking past it until you arrive at a street named Alta Loma Terrace, which ends at the back of a sad-looking parking lot. This is the site of "The Siege of Fort Anthony," an unhappy chapter in Hollywood.

In 1964, Stephen Anthony lived at 6655 Alta Loma Terrace with his wife and three children. When a group of Hollywood moguls decided to build a museum about Hollywood history on that very spot, they kicked out all of his neighbors. But Anthony refused to leave. Sheriff's deputies showed up to evict him, and Anthony, an ex-marine, greeted them at the door with some choice words and a loaded shotgun.

The standoff lasted for weeks, and wound up in court. Anthony lost the case, but he held his ground. He finally let in a couple of guys who claimed to be fellow sympathetic marines, but they turned out to be undercover deputies, who tackled him and dragged him out of his home. The house was razed the next morning.

The sad coda to the whole affair is that the museum project was so severely mismanaged, that it was never built, and the ugly spillover parking lot for the Hollywood Bowl was shrugged into existence.

Address 2178 High Tower Drive, Hollywood, CA 90068, +1 (323) 851-7270 | Getting there Bus 224 to Highland/Camrose | Hours Unrestricted | Tip The Hollywood Pilgrimage Memorial Monument, a huge white cross, can be seen from the top of this neighborhood. You can even walk up to the cross for a view back to the High Tower by crossing Cahuenga to the other side of the freeway, and hiking a short, steep trail.

36 The Hollywood Bowl
All-access pass to Daisy Dell

For over 100 years, the Hollywood Bowl has been one of the most prestigious places on the planet to perform. Not only is it home to the Los Angeles Philharmonic, one of the world's great orchestras, but renowned artists, including The Beatles, Yo-Yo Ma, and Ella Fitzgerald, have wowed audiences here for decades, and it remains one of the premiere venues to take in a concert under the stars.

What many of the artists and attendees may not realize, though, is that this legendary place is far more than just a great amphitheatre. Even locals may not know this open secret: when there are no performances happening, the beautiful Hollywood Bowl is actually a public park. At 8am on any given morning, you'll find intrepid athletes of all ages and abilities working up a sweat by running up and down the prodigious stairs of the audience section, or working out near the stage. By lunchtime, a few picnickers will have arrived to eat a meal and stroll through the lush grounds. There's even an annual pancake breakfast organized and attended by people from the neighborhood. Despite these activities, the Hollywood Bowl feels especially spacious and special when you're there during a quiet time.

There have been many architectural improvements through the years, with notable contributions from such luminaries as Frank Gehry and Lloyd Wright. The iconic silhouette of the bandshell is widely recognizable, but a big part of the magic is the location itself. Back in 1919, when the site was first purchased for the Hollywood Bowl, this 59-acre spot in the Cahuenga Pass was called Daisy Dell, and it was already a popular place to have a picnic and gaze out at the city.

You'll want to check out the calendar of concerts and events at the Hollywood Bowl, of course. But make a point of coming by the venue during the daytime too, and when there are no events scheduled, to work out or just to sit and enjoy the park.

Address 2301 N Highland Avenue, Hollywood, CA 90068, +1 (323) 850-2000, www.hollywoodbowl.com, information@laphil.org | Getting there Bus 224 to Highland/Odin or see website for shuttle bus information | Hours Daily 8am–3pm, see website for concert and event schedule | Tip Built for the 1984 Olympics, the Jerome C. Daniel Overlook offers a unique view of the Hollywood Bowl from above (7036 Mulholland Drive, www.mrca.ca.gov/parks).

37 — Hollywood Farmers' Market

Sunday abundance

Way back in May of 1991, a handful of optimistic farmers woke up extra early to take a special gamble on a Sunday morning. In those days, farmers markets weren't as popular as they are now, so as they set up their little stalls early on a rainy morning, smack dab in the middle of Hollywood, the farmers likely wondered if anyone would show up to sample their healthy and delicious wares. Lo and behold, a few shoppers came and discovered the exquisite oranges, tomatoes, and other delights, and the farmers decided to return the next week. From those humble beginnings has grown one of the largest and best farmers' markets around.

On any given Sunday, you're likely to see top chefs from all over Los Angeles, especially the East Side, where great restaurants are popping up all over. They'll be combing through the lush organic produce, meats, and seafood among over 160 vendors who set up in Hollywood every week. It's a smorgasbord of luscious edibles, crafts, and surprise treasures laid out for the throngs of Angelenos out enjoying the weekend.

This being Hollywood, of course there is also an impressive array of entertainment present each week. Some of the best musicians and performers in town provide the soundtrack to the joyful bustling of the Sunday shoppers. From kids' music, to bluegrass, to sophisticated jazz, you never know what you'll hear from week to week. Give yourself ample time to stop and enjoy the music tunes while you shop.

There are plenty of prepared foods available here as well. You'll find little coffee carts serving up perfect cappuccinos and lattes, street food of all kinds, and fully prepared meals fit for the finest restaurants. It's no wonder that crowds come out every Sunday – everyone from local families, to chefs on the prowl for the perfect seasonal ingredient finds what they're looking for at the Hollywood Farmers' Market.

Address 1600 Ivar Avenue, Hollywood, CA 90028, +1 (323) 463-3171, www.seela.org/markets-hollywood | Getting there Metro B to Hollywood/Vine (Red Line); bus 2 to Sunset/Ivar | Hours Sun 8am–1pm | Tip Hollywood is also home to the Original Farmer's Market, a unique mall that has been selling produce since the 1930s and is now filled with wonderful shops and restaurants (6333 W 3rd Street, www.farmersmarketla.com).

38 Hollywood Food Coalition
Doing good in the neighborhood

It's typically not the first thing that comes up in a conversation about Hollywood, but it's an undeniable fact that many in this town struggle to get enough to eat. Poverty is a big issue everywhere, but on these streets that we often associate with the glamour of the entertainment business, it can feel particularly surprising. There's one place that isn't looking the other way when it comes to helping out some of the most vulnerable people in the community. That place is the Hollywood Food Coalition.

The mission is simple: Make sure that the hungry get fed, and support those who are in need. It's a noble cause, and it's hard to overstate how good they are at striving towards their goal. Since 1987, they have not missed a single night of serving meals to hungry people in Hollywood.

There are several great programs that help people, so it's easy to get involved. One of the volunteer opportunities is to be a part of the most awesome community dinner in Hollywood. The amazing people at Hollywood Food Coalition feed people in Hollywood every single night of the year, rain or shine. That adds up to over 80,000 dinners annually. You can participate by volunteering for a shift, making a donation, or sharing another resource with people in Hollywood who are in need of some support.

While the community dinner is the longest-running program, there are many other ways that the Hollywood Food Coalition helps the Hollywood community. There are programs to donate clothing and blankets, others designed to connect people with all sorts of services, and so much more. They even partner with UCLA who hosts a mobile health clinic to provide medical services to those who couldn't otherwise access them. It's nice to know that while it's easy to enjoy Hollywood, it's also easy to make a contribution to the community to support residents who are having hard times.

Address 5939 Hollywood Boulevard, Hollywood, CA 90028, +1 (323) 462-2032, www.hofoco.org, info@hofoco.org | Getting there Metro B to Hollywood/Vine (Red Line); bus 180, 217 to Hollywood/Bronson | Hours Meal preparation volunteer hours Mon–Fri 1:30–5pm, Sat 2:30–6:30pm, Sun 3–6pm | Tip Stay in the giving spirit with another volunteer opportunity at Saint Stephens Church's food giveaway on Wednesday mornings (6125 Carlos Avenue, www.ststephenshollywood.org).

39_Hollywood Sculpture Garden

Yard art extravaganza

Don't be fooled into thinking that all of the magic and majesty in Hollywood exists only in the movies. In the shadow of the Hollywood Sign, with a view of the city below, is the Hollywood Sculpture Garden, a hidden treasure that will delight any who discover it.

Dr. Robby Gordon is a veterinarian, who lives in an unassuming neighborhood, but he's doing a lot more than taking care of people's pets. Dr. Gordon is also an artist, who has realized his longtime dream of turning the yard of his home into an unexpected and absolutely amazing sculpture garden. Over 100 dazzling sculptures from local, national, and even international artists adorn the yard/gallery, and it's well worth taking your time to wander through all of it. From the whimsical to the dramatic, you'll see pieces made of steel, glass, stone, bronze, and many other materials as well.

The garden itself isn't huge, but there are 138 sometimes-crooked stairs in the winding pathways, so be sure to wear your comfortable shoes and be ready for a bit of meandering as you hike around the yard on some uneven ground to take in the artwork and the view.

If you're a sculptor or an artist and you'd like to show your work in one of the most unconventional outdoor gallery spaces around, Gordon is always accepting online applications to join the more than 60 artists on exhibit. If you're not an artist, but you love outdoor art, you can actually rent the garden and host your own event there.

The paths and stairways are best explored by appointment, and if you're lucky, you might even get to chat with Dr. Gordon himself. But if you didn't get a chance to plan your visit in advance, don't worry. Just pull your car over to the side of the road as you head up to see the Hollywood Sign. You can usually wander quietly into the yard, or just look from the sidewalk, where there's still plenty to see.

Address 2430 Vasanta Way, Hollywood, CA 90068, +1 (949) 861-1709, www.hollywoodsculpturegarden.com, drrobbygordon@gmail.com | Getting there By car, from Franklin Avenue, north on N Beachwood Drive, left at Winans Drive, right at Vasanta Way | Hours Scheduled tours by reservation | Tip Down the road is International Woodwind, Laskar Reese's saxophone emporium. Serious sax enthusiasts should make an appointment because that's the only way to get in (2164 Vista Del Mar Avenue, www.internationalwoodwind.com).

40 __ Hollywood Toys & Costumes

The scariest toy store

If you are a believer in paranormal activity, then you probably already know that Hollywood is haunted. Even nonbelievers might find some of the unexplainable, ghostly happenings around town a little bit curious. The Roosevelt Hotel, Pantages Theatre, and of course the Hollywood Forever Cemetery are all famously and regularly visited by ghosts and weird occurrences. But one of Hollywood's haunted locations, where famous ghosts like Rudolph Valentino and Marilyn Monroe prefer to haunt the halls, is less well known than these legendary venues. It's Hollywood Toys and Costumes.

At first glance, it seems like a typical Hollywood Boulevard shop. Well, not quite typical. For one thing, it's massive. You will find 50,000 products available here, mostly dress-up oriented: wigs, costumes, masks, makeup, and anything else you might want for whatever makeover you have in mind. As you can imagine, Halloween is a very big deal here and has been ever since this place opened in 1950 as The Hollywood Toy Shop. It's not seasonal, though. This is an incredible place for all things costume-y all year round.

But it's not just the fabulous merchandise that makes this the most exciting toy store in Hollywood. The real thrill is in all of the poltergeists who haunt this place. It hasn't always been this way. When Hollywood Toys and Costumes moved to this location in 1995, they moved into a creepy building with a dark history that includes fires, murders and accidental deaths. Maybe that answers some of the perplexing questions that many employees ask. Why do certain items seem to leap off the shelves when nobody is around? Why do shadowy figures move through the aisles after closing? Why do boxes move around by themselves? Zac Bagans, the host of the *Ghost Adventures* TV show, called this "one of the creepiest and most poltergeist active buildings I've stepped foot inside…"

Address 6600 Hollywood Boulevard, Hollywood, CA 90028, +1 (800) 554-3444, www.hollywoodtoysandcostumes.com | Getting there Metro B to Hollywood/Highland (Red Line); bus 217 to Hollywood/Whitley | Hours Mon–Sat 10am–7pm, Sun 10:30am–7pm | Tip If you need a spicier costume, Hustler Hollywood has you covered. Or rather, uncovered (6540 Hollywood Boulevard, www.hustlerhollywood.com).

41 Hollywood United Methodist Church

Welcoming home for all

After construction was completed in March 1930, the Hollywood United Methodist Church (HUMC) was an instant icon. It had been modeled in part after London's Westminster Hall, and the majestic tower soared above Hollywood, demanding admiration. It soon became known as "the most famous church on the Pacific coast," and even members of the Wilcox family, who had founded Hollywood as their ranch, attended the congregation. The beautiful church was recognized by the city in 1983 and designated as a cultural-historical monument.

The look of the church is accentuated by an important added feature. In 1993, an enormous red ribbon was placed on the tower in recognition of World AIDS Day, and the 20-foot-high ribbon, impossible to miss, is still there today. At the time when it was first installed, it was a very bold statement. Many other churches were condemning the gay community, whom they blamed for the AIDS epidemic, and the HUMC wanted to send a very clear message: This church is a tireless advocate for gay rights and the queer community. The message was received loud and clear. So it's not a bit surprising that this has become a real home for LGBTQIA+ congregants.

There is ample Hollywood film history here, too. The church has been used in countless famous movies, including *Big Momma's House*, *Jarhead*, *People Like Us*, and many others. The gymnasium here is where the prom was held in *Back to the Future*, and the whole church was used as the set of *Sister Act*. It's also been used as a rehearsal space for many musical acts, including the Rockettes of Radio City Music Hall, who use the church to rehearse their annual holiday program.

Today, the church is busy with public and private programs, services, and events, infused with the kind of spirit that has endured for so many years.

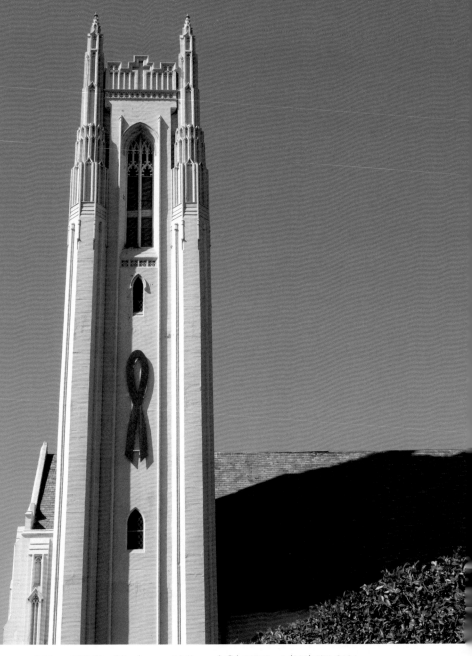

Address 6817 Franklin Avenue, Hollywood, CA 90028, +1 (323) 874-2104, www.hollywoodumc.org, info@hollywoodumc.org | Getting there Metro B to Hollywood/ Highland (Red Line); bus DASH Hollywood, 224 to Highland/Franklin | Hours See website for calendar of services and events | Tip Sunshine Glass is the perfect place to find beautiful art glass of all kinds (1556 N Highland).

42   Hollywood YMCA

The architecture of oppression

In 1921, a small YMCA was built in Hollywood. It had some rooms to sleep in, a gym, a "plunge pool," and a few other amenities. But by the mid-1920s, the burgeoning community needed a much bigger facility. A fundraising campaign took place to enlarge and redesign the Y, and everyone chimed in about it. A local clergy member even mentioned it during a sermon, saying "Hollywood would be better off with a Y than a fire department."

That's obviously a debatable statement, but the campaign was wildly successful, and the designer hired was none other than the great Paul Revere Williams, who was the first African American member of the American Institute of Architects. Williams had designed the African American 28th Street YMCA to great acclaim, and despite the rampant racism of the time, he was becoming known in Los Angeles for his work. What a troubling contradiction it must have been for him. Due to the practice of "redlining," which made it possible for banks to deny mortgages to Black people, it would have been nearly impossible for Williams to have purchased many of the properties he was designing. Yet there he was, being celebrated for his vision and craft, not only on buildings like post offices, courthouses, and YMCAs, but also on many dazzling homes for the Hollywood elite.

The redesign of the Hollywood Y relied on the same Spanish Colonial Revival style as the 28th Street YMCA and was duly praised at the time of its opening in 1928. It was also honored decades later with the distinction of being added to the National Registry of Historic Places.

This building now serves hundreds of Hollywood residents every day through the mission of the YMCA (and by being a great gym), and it's a beautiful reminder of a time in Hollywood where Paul Revere Williams broke through the barriers of racism to bring the gift of this building to the community.

Address 1553 N Schrader Boulevard, Hollywood, CA 90028, +1 (323) 467-4161, www.ymcala.org/locations/hollywood-ymca | **Getting there** Bus 2 to Sunset/Wilcox | **Hours** See website | **Tip** The Los Angeles LGBT Center, less than a block away, serves the community in so many ways, including performances of all kinds in their theater, and great art shows in their gallery (1625 N Schrader Boulevard, www.lalgbtcenter.org).

43 Hollywoodland Gates

A gateway to the past

According to local memory, the masons who did the stonework on the mighty gates of Hollywoodland were immigrants from Italy. They were friendly and focused, with a very high standard for their craft. That may explain why these majestic old towers, built in 1923, are still standing where the entrance to the famed development once stood, and why they were designated as a historic-cultural monument by the city of Los Angeles 40 years after they were constructed.

Originally, Hollywoodland was supposed to be a gated community, with guards stationed here to keep out the riff raff. There's even a belfry in one of the towers. Were the builders planning to announce visitors to the neighborhood by ringing a bell? Probably not, but it's an appealing look: sturdy and dignified, just the qualities the developers were looking for to define their fancy new neighborhood. The plan to put guards at the gates was never realized, as the stock market crash at the end of the decade put an end to that idea. But these two beautiful stone markers on either side of Beachwood Drive still stand sentinel – a gateway to another era.

The gates were designed by the lead architect of the subdivision, John DeLario, who also designed some of the most beautiful homes on the hills above, including the famous Castillo Del Lago, a magnificent palace of a house resembling an Italian villa. The gangster Bugsy Seigel lived there long before Madonna set up residence for a time. Allegedly, both famous residents left bullet holes in the finely crafted walls.

The gates have no such wounds. They stand proudly, making visitors feel welcome. Careful explorers will find other evidence of the stonemasons' craft here in the neighborhood. There are hidden stairways, overgrown retaining walls, and stone elements in gardens and homes that are sprinkled through the hills of Hollywoodland, waiting for you to discover them.

Address 2691 N Beachwood Drive, Hollywood, CA 90068 | Getting there Bus DASH Beachwood
Canyon to Beachwood/Westshire | Hours Unrestricted | Tip The 20,000-square-foot Castillo
Del Lago has been the site of many lurid and illicit happenings (6342 Mulholland Highway).

44 Holy Transfiguration Russian Orthodox Church

The onion domes of Hollywood

There are plenty of strange-looking things in Hollywood, but even here, the Holy Transfiguration Russian Orthodox Church stands out. You can see it from all over town, with its towering and beautiful onion domes. It's obviously a church to anyone who sees it, but it's more than just the amazing domes that make this place unique.

Like many churches, this one's foundation isn't just concrete and steel, but the rock-solid faith of its founding members. In the early 1930s, a handful of congregants of the Russian Orthodox community had the grand idea to build a big church that looked like the enormous ones in Russia. They were ambitious in their plans. Picture the Kremlin.

These early dreamers launched a campaign to garner donations for the project in 1935, but it didn't go very well. Two years later, they had only managed to raise a pathetic $638 measly dollars. All they could afford was a $500 down payment on an ugly $3000 double lot in Hollywood, of all places. Against better judgment, but with the sense that they had divine providence on their side, they bought the property where the church now stands.

And then supporters appeared. Church officials were discovered to have heretofore undisclosed carpentry skills. New donors appeared out of nowhere. And in May of 1944, just a few weeks before D-Day in Europe, the mortgage was paid off, the church was completed, and the domes soared above Hollywood, where they continue to welcome members today.

The church is absolutely gorgeous, with its soaring domes anointing the skies above Hollywood. It's striking on the inside as well, where you'll find the beautiful paintings and gilded iconography often seen in a Russian Orthodox Church, helping to make this place a stunning, inimitable icon of Hollywood architecture.

Address 5433 Fernwood Avenue, Hollywood, CA 90027, www.russianchurch.org, info@russianchurch.org | Getting there Bus DASH Hollywood to Fountain/Western | Hours See website for services and events | Tip Covenant House near the cathedral helps fight youth homelessness, which is a huge problem in Hollywood. You can donate, volunteer, or participate in an event (1325 N Western Avenue, www.covenanthousecalifornia.org).

45_Hotel Café

Where songwriters feel at home

The Hotel Café is neither a hotel, nor a café. It started as a coffee shop back in 2000, where you could get an espresso, a latte, or a bucket of ice. Why a bucket of ice? Well, back then they didn't have a liquor license, so if you decided to bring your own beer to one of the live music performances that were on offer, mostly in the acoustic artist vein, they were happy to sell you a way to keep your drinks cold. What the place lacked in terms of gear, permits, and other niceties, it made up for in great vibes and consistently good music. Pretty quickly, this became the quintessential place to see an up-and-coming singer songwriter. As such, the venue boasts a very impressive list of musical acts who played there early in their careers: Katy Perry, Billie Eilish, The Lumineers, John Mayer, Adele… the list is extremely long and ever growing.

These days, it looks and feels pretty much like any typical music venue, complete with two lovely stages, beautiful lighting, and great sound systems. But so many musicians feel that the venue is truly special that on some nights, there are as many talented artists in the shadows of the audience as there are in the spotlight up on the small stage. The fact that so many singers and songwriters call this place home really clicks with the warm, honest feel of the Hotel Café and might explain why there are lots of well-established artists who perform here, as well as those on the rise.

Over the years, there have been opportunities to see huge names, like Pete Townsend, Leonard Cohen, Weezer, and so many more, in a space that is far more intimate than the venues where such popular acts usually perform. So you never know if the artist who you see at the Hotel Café tonight might be performing at the Hollywood Bowl the next time they come to town. And you'll be able to say that you saw them play before they hit the big time.

Address 1623 1/2 N Cahuenga Boulevard, Hollywood, CA 90028, +1 (323) 461-2040, www.hotelcafe.com | Getting there Metro B to Hollywood/Vine (Red Line); bus 217 to Hollywood/Cahuenga | Hours See website for performance schedule | Tip The Fonda Theatre, another amazing music venue, is just four blocks away (6126 Hollywood Boulevard, www.fondatheatre.com).

46__Icons of Darkness
Biggest collection of creepy movie stuff

What happens to all of the screen-used costumes, props, and special effects when shooting for a movie is finished? Some undoubtedly wind up in the trash heap, some are recycled or repurposed for other productions, and maybe a few wind up going home surreptitiously with one of the performers or crew members. But luckily, an amazingly large amount seems to have wound up here, in the largest personal collection of scary movie stuff in the world.

Rich Correll was a child actor who appeared on *Leave It To Beaver*, back in 1960–1963, when the world was still in black and white. He went on to have an impressive career as a television producer and director, directing over 700 episodes of television shows, including many of the most successful sitcoms in history, like *Laverne and Shirley* and *Happy Days*. The whole time he was working in television, Rich was chasing another passion: collecting things from horror, sci-fi, and fantasy movies.

His entertainment industry connections had made him some interesting friendships and acquaintances, like Harold Lloyd, Boris Karloff, Alfred Hitchcock, and Peter Jackson. These relationships inspired Rich to honor the legacies of these Hollywood legends. They have also made it possible for the Icons of Darkness collection to acquire many one-of-a-kind items that will not be found anywhere else. The exhibit includes props, costumes, and various effects and doodads from dozens of films, including *The Terminator*, *Aliens*, *Star Wars*, *Jurassic Park*, *Harry Potter*, and so many more.

Whose bat suit is better: Christian Bale's or Michael Keaton's? How big is the T-Rex head from *Jurassic Park*? The half-hour tour of Icons of Darkness, guided by a knowledgeable docent, will answer all of your questions. If you love scary stuff, special effects, and just movies in general, this is one creepy and wonderful experience that you must not miss.

Address 6801 Hollywood Boulevard, Hollywood, CA 90028, +1 (323) 380-7548, www.iconsofdarkness.com, iconsofdarkness@gmail.com | Getting there Metro B to Hollywood/Highland (Red Line); bus 212, 217, 224 to Hollywood/Highland | Hours Sun–Thu 11am–9pm, Fri & Sat 11am–10pm | Tip Across the street is the Guinness World Records Museum, where you can see even more weird stuff (6764 Hollywood Boulevard, www.guinnessmuseumhollywood.com).

47 — The Janes House

Schoolhouse, service station, speakeasy

The oldest remaining house in Hollywood is hiding in plain sight in one of the most heavily trafficked places in the whole city. It's tucked into the back of a raucous courtyard with an outdoor bar and a steady stream of pedestrians walking by. You should take a closer look because this exquisite Queen Anne-style house was built all the way back in 1903, and has had a pretty storied history.

When it was first built, the house was just one in a whole development of large, hoity-toity Victorian homes, and the Janes family was delighted to move in. In 1911, the family opened a kindergarten in their house, and soon it was a full-fledged school. Kindergarteners through eighth graders studied here at The Misses Janes School of Hollywood, better known as simply the Janes House. It was extremely popular, especially after superstars like Charlie Chaplin, Douglas Fairbanks Sr., and Jesse Lasky started sending their children there. The school did quite well until the owners, also the teachers, died, and their four children struggled to make ends meet. Cars were beginning to be all the rage, so in 1926, they decided to set up a service station in front of the house and eventually rented some of the space in the yard for various shops to move in.

The property was named a landmark in 1982, but despite efforts to maintain it, it fell into serious disrepair. New owners moved the house to the back of the lot in 1985 and gave the front, which by then was basically a parking lot, a makeover with the same kind of beautiful and ornate styling as the house. It's the perfect setting for the 1920s-themed speakeasy that now occupies the house. The bar is called No Vacancy at Hotel Juniper, and it's a great place to dress up and have a drink in a setting that will take you right back to the turn of the last century, when the Janes House was really the Janes' house and speakeasies were romantic hideaways.

Address 1727 N Hudson Avenue, Hollywood, CA 90028, +1 (323) 465-1902, www.novacancyla.com, info@novacancyla.com | Getting there Metro B to Hollywood/ Vine (Red Line); bus DASH Hollywood to Hollywood/Wilcox | Hours Daily 8pm–2am | Tip If you like historic houses, get up into the hills to see the Fitzpatrick-Leland House, designed by Rudolph Schindler in 1936 (8078 Woodrow Wilson Drive).

48__Janis Joplin Shrine

The 27 Club lives on in Room 105

On October 4th, 1970, legendary singer Janis Joplin was 27 years old. Her music career had taken off, and she was one of the top rock stars in the world. "Piece of My Heart," her biggest hit, had launched her into stardom, but sudden fame proved to be too much for her to handle. The rock-and-roll lifestyle she personified would be her demise.

That night, she became a member of the "27 Club," a sad fraternity of rock stars who all perished at the same age and in much the same way. Janis joined Jimi Hendrix, Jim Morrison, Robert Johnson, and later Kurt Cobain and Amy Winehouse, by injecting heroin for the last time – a powerful dose that, when mixed with the alcohol she was drinking, turned lethal.

The unassuming room at the Landmark Garden Hotel on Franklin Avenue, where her body was discovered, is now the object of many fan pilgrimages. The name of the hotel has changed (it's now the Highland Gardens), but fans can still spend a night in the famous Room 105, which now has an extensive graffiti-style shrine filled with art, lyrics, and musings from fans and friends, drawn on the hallway and closet walls. This is the place to commune with Joplin's spirit and remember her powerful voice.

Years have passed, but the moment seems all too present. Pulling into the parking lot, it's easy to imagine her psychedelically painted Porsche parked in its usual spot. There's a fresh coat of paint in the lobby now, but you can imagine Janis wobbling down the hall to the cigarette machine that tragic night, mere minutes away from death, drugs already coursing through her veins. As you open the door to Room 105, you feel the weight of the scene as though it was still there, her crumpled body too silent, and the awful truth brand new.

"Long live Rock & Roll," says one of the scrawled memorials on the wall in Janis' closet. Long live Janis, and the rest of the 27 Club too.

Address 7047 Franklin Avenue, Hollywood, CA 90028, +1 (323) 850-0536, www.highlandgardenshotel.com | **Getting there** Bus 212, 217 to Hollywood/Sycamore | **Hours** Unrestricted from outside or by reservation for Room 105 | **Tip** If you're making a sad tour of rock 'n' roll death sites, Hollywood is also where Dee Dee Ramone accidentally overdosed. Sing a tribute on the sidewalk outside the apartment building, but don't disturb the occupants (6740 Franklin Place).

49__Japan House

Japanese art and culture

In Los Angeles, like many cities around the world, there is a strong Japanese influence. It's not surprising, considering that this city has one of the largest populations of Japanese residents anywhere in the United States. There's Little Tokyo, home to the Japanese American National Museum, Japanese gardens from Pasadena to the west side, and, of course, the hundreds of delicious sushi joints all over town.

But there's only one spot in the whole city that is an actual project of the Japanese Government's Ministry of Foreign Affairs, and it's right in the heart of Hollywood: Japan House. Covering more than 14,000 square feet on two different floors of the Ovation Shopping Center, this is a place where you'll want to take your time.

Each section of Japan House is a curated experience designed to highlight elements of Japanese culture. The second floor features the WAZA shop and exhibition halls, and the fifth floor is where you'll find the library, restaurant, and salon, each offering a unique way of seeing, tasting, and learning about Japanese culture. The WAZA shop sells all kinds of beautiful products representing various aspects, including fashion, food, and technology. The library at Japan House is filled with Manga, photography and many other books, including a section detailing Japanese culture in Los Angeles. The salon/event space and exhibition galleries are always bustling with potent content that takes a deep dive into architecture, design, film, art, so keep your eye on the "Happenings" schedule here.

The restaurant upstairs isn't a run-of-the-mill eatery, but rather an immersive and enlightening experience that connects Japanese cuisine with the exhibits happening downstairs in the galleries. You can look at the art and history first, then go upstairs to taste the related foods, and look out at the beautiful view over the city, where Japanese culture has been so important.

Address 6801 Hollywood Boulevard, Level 2 & Level 5, Hollywood, CA 90028, +1 (800) 516-0565, www.japanhousela.com | Getting there Metro B to Hollywood/ Highland (Red Line) | Hours Mon–Fri 11am–7pm, Sat & Sun 11am–8pm | Tip To take in more Japanese art and culture, visit the nearby Japan Pavilion at the Los Angeles County Museum of the Arts (5905 Wilshire Boulevard, www.lacma.org).

50_John Sowden House

Dark secrets of the Black Dahlia house

Hollywood has a lot of spectacular and famous homes, but none with so sordid a story as the infamous Sowden House. This architectural masterpiece was built in 1926 in neo-Mayan style by Lloyd Wright, son of the legendary Frank Lloyd Wright, for his friend, artist and photographer John Sowden. The house itself is incredibly striking. A stunning façade and carefully appointed interiors lead from one breathtaking room to the next. The inner courtyard is modeled after an actual Mayan temple in the Yucatán, and just as temples of that era were known for the blood offerings in which a living creature was sacrificed, so too is the Sowden House known for killing.

In the 1940s, this was the home of Dr. George Hodel, a well-known and admired physician in Los Angeles. Although he wasn't named in the investigation at the time, he is now known as the prime suspect in the grisly 1947 murder of Elizabeth Short – aka the Black Dahlia. Hodel's own son Steve, now a retired LAPD detective, began to investigate the Black Dahlia murder in order to clear his father's name, but he soon discovered much damning evidence that changed his mind. He came to believe that his father not only killed and dismembered Short, but actually killed *many others* at this house as well, and may have buried some of their bodies here. Hodel insists, in the many books that he's written on the subject, that his father was in fact the notorious Zodiac killer as well.

We may never know the truth about Dr. Hodel and the Black Dahlia. The beautiful house is often used for filming and has appeared in many movies, but for some reason, it has never been properly investigated. So, when you visit the Sowden House for one of the many private and charity events that are held here, just know that there may be ghosts drifting up from the basement, where untold horrors may or may not have occurred.

Address 5121 Franklin Avenue, Hollywood, CA 90027, www.sowdenhouse.com | Getting there Bus DASH Hollywood to Franklin/Normandie | Hours Unrestricted from outside only | Tip If you decide to make a movie about the murder, the Cop Prop Shop two blocks over is where you can browse by appointment, and rent the law enforcement look for your shoot (1751 N Alexandria Avenue, www.coppropshop.com).

51 Johnny Ramone's Party

Hollywood Forever Cemetery, underground club

The Hollywood Forever Cemetery is the final resting place of dozens of Hollywood notables who knew how to enjoy a good party. So it makes sense that this cemetery throws one heck of a bash. The biggest blowout of the year is *Día De Los Muertos*, featuring Aztec dancers, multiple stages, and upwards of 35,000 enthusiastic revelers, who pack the grounds to build elaborate altars honoring deceased loved ones. But that's just the start. This rollicking graveyard screens movies (on the side of a mausoleum, naturally) and hosts a concert series with big acts like Arctic Monkeys, Modest Mouse, and the appropriately named Death Cab for Cutie.

One night a year is reserved for the Johnny Ramone memorial, where any number of rock'n'roll luminaries take the stage to celebrate the revered punk rock icon. Henry Rollins, Rose McGowan, Billie Joe Armstrong, The Red Hot Chili Peppers, and many more have participated in the festivities, all to raise money for cancer research. Be sure to stop by Johnny's grave afterwards – the statue of him shredding on his guitar is one of the coolest markers in the entire place. That's saying a lot when there are graves boasting fountains, rocket ships, and even live peacocks.

With all of its entertainment offerings, the Hollywood Forever Cemetery isn't exactly a secret, but it does hold one particular secret itself: this place is extremely haunted. Pay careful attention, and you may see the mysterious "woman in black," a ghost who regularly brings flowers to the grave of Rudolph Valentino. Could she be the spirit of the once-living woman in black who brought him flowers? Perhaps death didn't end her devotion. She's been spotted so often that now there is an annual Valentino memorial event that draws an entire crowd of women dressed in black.

Whether you want to party or mourn, this is where to go to see your favorite stars in one place.

Address 6000 Santa Monica Boulevard, Hollywood, CA 90038, +1 (866) 706-4826, www.hollywoodforever.com, info@hollywoodforever.com | Getting there Metro B to Hollywood/Vine (Red Line); bus 4 DASH Hollywood to Gower/Santa Monica | Hours See website for events calendar | Tip Paramount Studios is right next door on land purchased from the cemetery and offers a 2-hour studio tour every day and a 4.5-hour VIP tour on weekdays (5515 Melrose Avenue, www.paramountstudiotour.com).

52 Jumbo's Clown Room

Female-owned bikini bar badassery

You can't always believe the outrageous stories you hear about celebrity sightings in Hollywood. But if someone ever tells you that they once sipped a delicious, no frills cocktail with the legendary Lemmy Kilmister from Motörhead at a retro clown-themed strip joint, well, the story is probably true. That's just the way things happen when you walk into Jumbo's Clown Room.

This place is one sexy circus, and Lemmy's not the only celebrity who hung out here. Charles Bukowski used to be a regular as well, and so did Anthony Bourdain. David Lynch is rumored to have written most of *Blue Velvet* while sitting right here at the bar. On any given night, there's no telling who you might bump into in this kitschy but cool Hollywood hang.

But the prospect of seeing famous people isn't what makes this place so great. Maybe it's the fact that Jumbo's is owned and operated by women (yes, of course it matters). It could be the feeling of being in the world's greatest neighborhood bar that's made possible by the awesome jukebox cranking out The Cramps or Black Sabbath. Perhaps it's the chatty bartenders and approachable performers making everyone feel at home. Whatever the reason, Jumbo's patrons tend to be both women and men "that wish to clown around," and who don't seem to be imbued with as much of the sleaze factor that prevails in other strip joints.

The dancers here have always been known as edgy, empowered, athletic, and fun. Case in point: rock goddess Courtney Love herself danced here back in the day. It's no different today. The performers are diverse, super talented, hot as hell, and basically badass. Drinks are reasonably priced, there's no cover charge, and it's a tiny little room filled with strippers, retro clown décor, and maybe a celebrity or two ... what more could you ask? This is a magnificent, family-owned business run by women who take their clowning seriously.

Address 5153 Hollywood Boulevard, Hollywood, CA 90027, +1 (323) 666-1187, www.jumbos.com, info@shopjumbos.com | Getting there Metro B to Hollywood/Western (Red Line); bus 180, 206, 217 to Hollywood/Normandie | Hours Wed – Sun 8pm – 2am | Tip If you leave Jumbo's by 1am, stop by the House of Pies for a delicious dessert or late-night breakfast (1869 N Vermont Boulevard, www.houseofpiesla.com).

53 Karnevil
Sexy birthday freak show

The terrifying clown is absolutely gigantic. It looms over the entire bar, grinning menacingly down at the patrons as though they are about to be his snacks. The room is filled with spooky mist, through which the colorful lights of a carnival sideshow blink and shimmer ominously. Why then, in this slightly nightmare-ish setting, are these people laughing uproariously and seemingly having such a fantastic time? Because this is Karnevil, where the dark circus theme is all part of one of the most enjoyable nights out in all of Hollywood.

The talent is top notch, featuring all manner of acrobats, magicians, and freak show standouts. These performers, including aerial contortionists, fire eaters, jugglers, hand balancers, and more, are among the best circus acts anywhere, and this setting is an absolutely amazing place to experience them. You'll enjoy a fabulous dinner – or brunch, if you prefer – filled with carnival-inspired eats and drinks, and a show like no other, especially if you're here for a birthday, in which case you definitely will be dragged onstage and treated to a truly immersive show. Your evening will be very funny, a little scary, super sexy, and an all-around great time.

Yes, it's a familiar formula: dinner and a show. But Karnevil adds the excitement and thrill that comes along with dangerous, scary stunts and talented, sexy performers taking it all up a few rungs. Burlesque, Vaudeville, and *American Horror Story* all rolled into one. If you're already a circus lover, then this place will be right up your alley. But don't be deterred if circuses aren't usually your thing. If you're just in the mood for a rock-solid, grown-up show that's somehow edgy and hot while being simultaneously hilarious and inspiring, step into the tent and brace yourself for the experience ahead. Watch out for the big menacing clown, order some five-star carnival treats, and enjoy Karnevil.

Address 6627 Hollywood Boulevard, Hollywood, CA 90028, +1 (323) 333-8858, www.karnevilla.com, info@karnevilla.com | Getting there Metro B to Hollywood/Highland (Red Line); bus 217 to Hollywood/Whitley | Hours See website for showtimes | Tip Right next door is hip hop club Ballet Hollywood, where you can keep the party going all night long (6623 Hollywood Boulevard, www.ballethollywood.com).

54__ The Kibitz Room
Rock 'n' roll deli

Yes, Canter's deli has an absolutely delicious bowl of matzo ball soup. Sure, the pastrami sandwich was named "Number One Best" by *The Los Angeles Times*. And everyone knows, the chocolate chip rugelach is to die for. But believe it or not, the fantastic and enormous menu at Canter's, filled with yummy deli foods, isn't the coolest reason to stop in.

Originally from New Jersey, Canter's has been in Los Angeles since 1931 and at its current location on Fairfax since 1953. But it wasn't until the opening of The Kibitz Room, a cocktail lounge attached to the restaurant that this place cemented its legacy as the coolest rock 'n' roll deli in town.

The Kibitz Room opened in 1961, serving cocktails and presenting live musical performances. By that time, rock stars and celebrities of all kinds were already hanging out at Canter's. It wasn't unusual to see Marilyn Monroe eating here, or members of the Doors. It's only a half a mile from the Sunset Strip, after all, where many performances were happening. And there's another feature that makes it the best place for a late-night hang: Canter's is open 24 hours a day. It only closes twice a year for two Jewish holidays, Rosh Hashanah and Yom Kippur. And what do rock stars and other celebs do when they stay up all night at the deli? They kibitz, of course. "Kibitz" is a Yiddish word that means "chitchat." Hence the name.

From the early 1960s until today, there has been a musical act at the Kibitz Room every night. Famous names often pop up or sit in. Guns N' Roses, Joni Mitchell, and the Red Hot Chili Peppers have appeared here, among many others. And many more stars have come for a drink or a corned beef sandwich, or to hear the music, or just to sit and kibitz. There's no guarantee that you'll see Taylor Swift, Mick Jagger, or Barack Obama here. But they have indeed been spotted here before.

Address 419 N Fairfax Avenue, Hollywood, CA 90036, +1 (323) 651-2030, www.cantersdeli.com/kibitz-room | Getting there Bus DASH Fairfax, 217, 218 to Fairfax/Oakwood | Hours Daily 10:30pm–1:40am | Tip The Bagel Broker, one block away, has the best bagels in the neighborhood, which is saying something (7825 Beverly Boulevard, www.bagelbroker.com).

55__Kulak's Woodshed

Music webcast from Grandma's TV studio

Jackson Browne and Paula Cole have played here. So have guitar legend Albert Lee and other giants of the music industry. Hundreds of artists speak of it with great affection. So why has such a beloved venue as Kulak's Woodshed wallowed for so long in obscurity? It's certainly not due to lack of care from the owner and founder Paul Kulak. He has poured his heart, soul, and a lot of his own money into this place.

When he opened in 1999, Kulak insisted that this little storefront music venue would remain true to some key values, starting with no cover charge. "When you go to grandma's house, you don't get hit with a door charge," he says. Dogs are allowed in. Finally, there's no interrupting the music with food or drink.

This tiny place is festooned with all kinds of cozy bric-a-brac, as if Grandma's house exploded, flinging all the quilts, stuffed animals, newspaper articles, and tchotchkes into every corner. It only seats 50 people or so in mismatched chairs, sofas, and one big bed. Musicians play for free, Paul and some friends work as volunteers, and everyone has an amazing time – and then goes broke. Yes, there's a donation bucket that goes around, but it usually fails to cover the basic costs. So be as generous as you can.

Kulak's is located on Laurel Canyon, where the kind of music that is regularly heard here had its heyday in the 1970s. But you don't actually need to be in the room to enjoy the shows. Paul decided early on that the music was too good not to share it. So he installed a whole system of cameras, built some tracks out of some old skateboards and spare parts, and turned the place into a legitimate television studio. Every single performance is broadcast live on the web, with six cameras, top notch sound and lighting, and a volunteer reading emails from viewers around the world. When you come to Kulak's, put a big donation into the bucket and keep the dream alive.

Address 5230 Laurel Canyon Boulevard, North Hollywood, CA 91607, +1 (818) 766-9913, www.kulakswoodshed.com | Getting there Bus 230 to Laurel Canyon/G Line | Hours See website for performance schedule | Tip Grab some of the best tacos in town on the way to the show at Hugo's Tacos (4749 Coldwater Canyon Avenue, www.hugostacos.com).

56 La Bicicocina

The kitchen where you can whip up a bike

Hollywood, like all of greater Los Angeles, is a car-obsessed town. Imagine your favorite movie star rolling in a convertible with the California breeze blowing through their perfect hair, passing palm trees and paparazzi, oozing sensuality, and stopping your heart with a wink. In reality, though, thousands of cars cruise up and down the boulevards at all hours, clogging the roads, growling and roaring into the ears of all who visit, and belching noxious fumes into everyone's lungs. But some in Hollywood know that there is a better way.

La Bicicocina, or the Bicycle Kitchen, is an all-volunteer nonprofit organization that is dedicated to teaching people the joys of pedal-powered transportation. This is the place where you can learn how to care for your bike, from regular maintenance, to changing flat tires, to building a project bike from donated parts. You can't buy a new bicycle here, but your very own crazy-looking Frankenstein-cycle is going to be way cooler anyway.

Founded in 2002, La Bicicocina moved around for a decade, avoiding rising rents and outgrowing spaces as its popularity grew. In 2012, it successfully raised the funds to buy its own building on Fountain Avenue, where it has been ever since. The Kitchen is filled with tools for anyone to come by and use. There's a suggested donation of $8 per hour, but nobody is ever turned away for lack of funds. There's always a volunteer "cook" available to help out and share knowledge about bike mechanics. Don't get the wrong idea: this is not a bike shop. They won't fix your flat tire for you, but they will teach you how to repair it yourself.

Come get your hands dirty – this is one kitchen where you don't need to wash up before you get started. Start a bicycle project, or just tune up your ride when you're biking through Hollywood. The only thing you won't find here is a parking lot.

Address 4429 Fountain Avenue, Hollywood, CA 90029, +1 (323) 662-2776, www.bicyclekitchen.org | Getting there Metro B to Vermont/Sunset (Red Line); bus 182 to Fountain/Virgil | Hours Tue & Wed 6–9pm, Sat noon–4pm | Tip Hop on your bike and head up Hillhurst Avenue to The Best Fish Taco in Ensenada, which, as advertised, has amazing fish tacos (1650 Hillhurst Avenue, www.bestfishtacoinensenada.com).

57 La Luz de Jesus Gallery
Lowbrow art mecca

In 1971, Barbara and Henry "Hank" Shire and their family opened a shop called The Soap Plant, to little fanfare. The whole eccentric gang was involved, selling homemade soap, original ceramics made by their (now renowned) ceramicist and sculptor son Peter, and hand-crafted leather made by their other artist son Billy, who, thanks to *Art Forum Magazine*, became known in the art world as "the Peggy Guggenheim of Lowbrow." Barbara and Hank were both artists as well, and before too long, the store grew to include Wacko, a pop culture toy shop with a punk rock sensibility and bit of a cult following.

It wasn't until 1986 that Billy Shire launched La Luz de Jesus gallery at the back of the Soap Plant/Wacko complex, which is considered by many to be the birthplace of the lowbrow art movement. The focus of the gallery has always been on folk, outsider, kitschy, and/or deviant art genres. The legions of fans, new art collectors, and celebrities who are drawn to the gallery are proof of the potency of the approach.

The term "lowbrow" may sound derisive, and it might even be sneered at by some of the art world elite, but it's intended to be inclusive and accessible. By embracing pop culture – tattoos, religious ephemera, rock and roll, Hollywood iconography, comic books, surfing, and so much more – La Luz de Jesus launched the Lowbrow movement, and it is still the go-to place to discover eclectic new artists.

They've changed locations a couple of times since those early days, but the store and gallery are still going strong on Hollywood Boulevard. And an art opening at La Luz de Jesus is still the center of the lowbrow art universe, where you may meet well-known artists, scenesters, and celebs, alongside some of the coolest punky art fans and collectors around. It's the only gallery with a full-blown novelty/pop art/bookstore, and it's well worth a visit.

Address 4633 Hollywood Boulevard, Hollywood, CA 90027, +1 (323) 666-7667, www.laluzdejesus.com | **Getting there** Metro B to Vermont/Sunset (Red Line) | **Hours** Mon–Sat 11am–7pm, Sun 11am–6pm | **Tip** If you're feeling inspired by the art in the gallery, pop into Blue Rooster Art Supplies, right next door (4661 Hollywood Boulevard, www.blueroosterart.com).

58 La Monarca Mexican Bakery

Saving butterflies is delicious

The monarch butterfly is an endangered species. So many California residents are planting butterfly-friendly gardens to help the monarch bounce back from the brink. Year after year, though their population is shrinking, the beautiful creatures keep going, intent on survival and migrating over 3,000 miles twice each year between Canada and Mexico.

It's that same spirit of resiliency, courage, and ambition that inspired two immigrants from Monterrey, Mexico in 2005. Ricardo Cervantes and Alfredo Livas had met at business school in California, and they wanted to start a business that was connected to where they grew up. To the great benefit of hungry folks all over Los Angeles, they decided to open a little *panaderia* named after the embattled monarch. The partners had assessed that, just like the decline of the beautiful butterfly, there was also a shortage of yummy Mexican baked goodies in Los Angeles, and they intended to build a bridge between the two cultures. La Monarca opened in 2006, and the rest is delicious history. It's now a small chain, bringing Oaxacan coffee, luscious pan dulce, and dozens of other treats to Hollywood and beyond.

Cervantes and Livas are not only committed to bringing "the sweet flavor of Mexico" to Los Angeles, but they're also giving back to the community. Part of their mission is to create opportunities in underserved areas, and they also make an effort to use only natural ingredients in all of their goodies, without preservatives or artificial flavors or colors. And the lovely but endangered Monarch? A percentage of every dollar earned at La Monarca goes to Ecolife Conservation, whose programs protect and preserve the butterfly.

So if you reside in their migratory path, go out and plant some milkweed for the monarchs to eat along their journey. But also know that when you bite into that delicious pastry, you're also doing your part.

Address 1096 N Western Avenue, Hollywood, CA 90029, +1 (323) 498-0211, www.lamonarcabakery.com | Getting there Bus 4 to Santa Monica/Western | Hours Mon–Sat 6am–9pm, Sun 6am–8pm | Tip Across the street is Gower Gulch, a Western-themed strip mall where actual cowboys used to congregate between takes while making Western movies in the early days of film (6122 Sunset Boulevard).

59__Largo at the Coronet
New vibe in a classic theater

As a music and comedy venue, Largo has been around since 1989, first as a 100-seat club on Fairfax, then upgrading to the larger and more historic Coronet Theatre in 2008. But the Coronet has a storied history of presenting groundbreaking work that still seems to infuse the shows today.

In 1947, the Coronet opened with a world premiere of a Bertolt Brecht play, *Galileo*, featuring Charles Laughton, and quickly established itself as a cutting edge, serious presenter. The next two shows, *Skin of Our Teeth* by Thornton Wilder and *No Exit* by Jean-Paul Sartre, were not only hits, but industry-shaking masterworks. As the decades passed, there were more than 300 theatrical productions, as well as avant-garde films, and the theater thrived for a time.

By the 1970s though, the theater was mainly screening porn, and the clientele had largely changed. They continued to produce plays as well, but the tone was different. In 1976, movie star Sal Mineo left a rehearsal at the theater and was stabbed to death by a mugger. The tragedy didn't put an end to the Coronet, but it just wasn't the same.

The place changed hands a few times in the 1980s and 1990s. It was taken over in 2008 by Largo, where mind-blowing musical and comedic performances are the standard, and luminaries of the industry perform, often in long residencies. On any night of the week, you'll be treated to a show featuring stars like Tig Notaro or Aimee Mann, and there will likely be surprise guests that create some "only at the Largo" moments. Where else will you see a pairing like Zach Galifianakis and Fiona Apple, and in a theater that seats fewer than 300 people?

Each beautiful moment at Largo hearkens back to the Coronet's roots. There are no cell phones allowed here. This is a place to be present and really tune in to the performers. For that reason, it's truly loved by artists and patrons alike.

Address 366 N La Cienega Boulevard, Hollywood, CA 90046, www.largo-la.com, largonews@gmail.com | Getting there Bus DASH Fairfax, 105 to La Cienega/Beverly | Hours See website for performance and event calendar | Tip The Greenway Court Theatre hosts Da Poetry Lounge, an open-mic poetry night on Tuesdays, and a myriad of offering on other nights (544 N Fairfax Avenue, www.greenwaycourttheatre.org).

60 Lasky-Demille Barn
Studio in a barn

A large sign on the front of the Hollywood Heritage Museum proudly proclaims that the Lasky-Demille Barn, where the museum is housed, was established in 1913. That's sort of true, but like a lot of Hollywood lore, there's more to the story of this important barn that has moved all around Hollywood.

The barn was actually built ca. 1895, as a simple stable for Col. Robert Northam, who owned a huge chunk of land in Hollywood at the time. He sold the place to Jacob Stern a couple of years later, who in turn rented it out to a couple of enterprising young guys, who wanted to get into the brand-new business of movie making. In 1911, the humble little barn became one of the first-ever movie studios, where Louis L. Burns and Harry Revier did everything from writing scripts to putting on costumes and makeup, to developing and editing the films.

Their big break came in 1913 – hence the sign on the front of the barn – when Burns and Revier met Jesse Lasky, Cecil B. DeMille, and Samuel Goldwyn, all of whom would go on to become titans of the Hollywood film industry. The Lasky Company leased the studio and set about making the first feature film, Cecil B. DeMille's *The Squaw Man*. That film helped set the course of movie history and cemented the legacy of the studio in a barn.

The entire building was picked up and moved to a new site in 1926, to where Paramount Studios stand today. The barn was used as Paramount's gym for a bunch of years, and it was shuffled around the lot there a few times, where it appeared in several movies and the hit television series *Bonanza*. In 1979, the barn was moved to a parking lot, where it resided until 1982, when it went to its current location and became the Hollywood Heritage Museum. There's an enormous collection of Hollywood photographs and memorabilia here, and you can even see a recreation of DeMille's private office.

Address 2100 N Highland Avenue, Hollywood, CA 90068, +1 (323) 874-2276, www.hollywoodheritage.org | Getting there Bus 224 to Highland/Milner or Highland/Camrose | Hours Fri–Sun 11am–3pm | Tip The Ford Theatre, built in 1920, is a more intimate version of the Hollywood Bowl. At only 1,200 seats, every one is the best seat in the house (2580 Cahuenga Boulevard E, www.theford.com).

61 Marilyn's Footprints
Tiny giant shoes to fill

The TLC Chinese Theatre, formerly Grauman's, just might be the most famous movie theater on the globe. Many of the world's biggest movies have their premieres here, with fans flocking to catch a glimpse of their favorite stars. At the grand opening in 1927, where the Cecil B. DeMille film *King of Kings* was screened for the first time, thousands of people crowded Hollywood Boulevard, and a riot broke out as the horde fought for a chance to see the celebrities.

Now events are mostly civil, but the fans still come out in droves. There are usually costumed performers out front, and the courtyard is still filled with the prints of the famous hands and feet of some of the biggest names from Hollywood's Golden Age, immortalized in the concrete. There are even horseshoe prints (thanks to Roy Rogers and Trigger), cigars (George Burns and Groucho Marx), Harpo's bare feet, and some nose prints. Even Marilyn Monroe, at the height of her stardom, left her indelible impression here.

In June 1953, Marilyn Monroe and Jane Russell, stars of the movie *Gentlemen Prefer Blondes*, pressed their hands and feet into the wet cement in front of the TLC Chinese Theatre, joining dozens of movie stars who were already immortalized there. Ten years earlier, when Betty Grable, known for her shapely legs, was being honored, she had drawn a leg print instead of using her feet. Seeing that approach, Marilyn reportedly quipped that she ought to sit in the cement, and Jane should lie down on her belly in it, to immortalize their most famous, ahem, assets.

Don't bother looking because they didn't do the racy stunt, but you can still stand where they once did. Marilyn's legend is larger than life, but her itty bitty footprints (reportedly, she wore a size six shoe, but perhaps they're even a bit smaller?) have made many aspiring actresses feel like Bigfoot when they've tried to fill her shoes.

Address 6925 Hollywood Boulevard, Hollywood, CA 90028, +1 (323) 461-3331, www.tclchinesetheatres.com, manager@chinesetheatres.com | **Getting there** Metro B to Hollywood/Highland (Red Line); bus 212, 217 to Hollywood/Highland | **Hours** Scheduled tours by reservation only | **Tip** Marilyn fans will want to walk one block east to peek into the Hollywood Wax Museum to see her life-sized effigy (6767 Hollywood Boulevard, www.hollywoodwaxentertainment.com).

62 Mashti Malone's
Ice cream in the happiness business

Hollywood has many one-of-a-kind spots – that's part of what makes this town so special. And this spot may be the world's only ice cream parlor with a half-Iranian, half-Irish name.

The curiosity of the name and signage at Mashti Malone's is easily explained. Mashti Sirvani immigrated to the US during the Iranian Revolution and worked as a chef in a Persian restaurant. It was a natural job for him, having been raised in Iran in a family of restaurateurs. But he wanted to be "in the happiness business," and luckily, his real passion was ice cream. He was eventually able to pull together the funds to buy an ice cream shop, and the happiness business was underway.

The storefront he bought in Hollywood was called Mugsy Malone's, and it sported a large sign out front with a big green shamrock on it. Sirvani knew that he wanted a different name, but he couldn't afford to change the entire sign … and there you have it! That insolvency/ stroke of genius birthed the amazing Mashti Malone's. The shamrock stayed, including the good luck it brought.

And it worked. Mashti Malone's has been a huge hit in Hollywood since it opened in 1982, and with good reason: the ice cream is fantastic! Incredible flavors like ginger rosewater, cherry *faloodeh*, and Persian cucumber are served up alongside old standards, including vanilla and chocolate. If you're adventurous, you'll definitely want to try the *faloodeh*, which is an amazing concoction containing rice noodles and possibly magical fairy dust – how else can it taste so good? If you're more of a traditionalist, the vanilla is actually heavenly as well. The flavors are constantly changing and evolving, so there's always a good reason to come back for more.

Empty pockets rarely have a silver lining, but they did for this entrepreneur of happiness and for everyone who stops in for scoops of this delicious, creamy goodness.

Address 1525 N La Brea Avenue, Hollywood, CA 90028, +1 (323) 874-6168,
www.mashtimalone.com, mmalone@mashtimalone.com | Getting there Bus 2, 212
to Sunset/La Brea | Hours Sun–Thu 11am–11:30pm, Fri & Sat 11am–midnight |
Tip Charlie Chaplin had some adorable, storybook-like bungalows built in 1923
to house crew members working at his nearby studio (1330 N Formosa Avenue).

63 Medieval Torture Museum

Misery, pain, and selfies

There are many unique museums in Hollywood. If you want to see cars, head to the Petersen Automotive Museum. If you like movies, try the Academy Museum of Motion Pictures. But if you're fascinated by dark, creepy things, and you want a close look at the horrific history of humans being awful to one another, there's the Medieval Torture Museum. It sounds weird, and rest assured, it is. It's interactive, but don't get the wrong idea. You won't be literally torturing anyone, and the only scars you'll leave with will be emotional ones from contemplating the cruelty of the various torments depicted here.

The exhibits are gruesome but presented with a slightly campy, tongue-ever-so-slightly-in-cheek kind of attitude. Joining in the torture is part of the fun here. Turn the cranks on machines that break bones, pull the ropes on swinging pendulum blades, and, of course, throw your friends in the stockades and take selfies. This museum has a scary vibe that's part Halloween and part social studies.

Accompanying each horrific device, culled from private collections of aficionados who must be some rather unusual individuals, is a description of how each particular torture is administered, and for which transgressions. Public drunkenness? You're immersed in a barrel of cold water, or disgustingly worse, with only your head out, you're then placed in the public square to endure the horrible whims of your fellow citizens. Is your crime Adultery? Witchcraft? The punishments are too awful to describe here, but finding out is well worth the price of admission for those with a strong constitution.

The Medieval Torture Museum manages to make something truly awful into something that's both educational and fun. The tone of the experience is captured perfectly on a T-shirt that you'll find for sale in the gift shop: "Medieval Torture Museum – I Hope You Step On A Lego."

Address 6757 Hollywood Boulevard, Hollywood, CA 90028, +1 (213) 414-7777, www.medievaltorturemuseum.com | Getting there Metro B to Hollywood/Highland (Red Line); bus 212, 217, 224 to Hollywood/Highland | Hours Sun–Thu 10am–10pm, Fri & Sat 10am–midnight | Tip If you need a break after so much torture, you may want to book an appointment at Ole Henriksen Spa for both physical and spiritual recovery (8622 W Sunset Boulevard, www.olehenriksenspa.com).

64 Melrose Trading Post

Sunday flea market

Every Sunday from 9am to 5pm, the campus of Fairfax High School is transformed into the hippest flea market in Hollywood – and beyond. Those in the know line up early to be the first thrifty customers to pick through the week's treasures. If you're looking to find the trendiest, sexiest, coolest bits of vintage clothing, you'll see it right here, being worn by the inimitable vendors and shoppers at the Melrose Trading Post. Of course they're wearing it! But don't worry: they bought that saucy retro wardrobe they're rocking right here last Sunday. You can upgrade your look for next week too.

The school itself has had loads of famous alumni, as you'd expect from a Hollywood institution such as this one. You'll be stomping around the grounds of a public school that birthed such greats as Slash from Guns N' Roses and Flea from the Red Hot Chili Peppers, who are both too cool to even have last names. Many other musicians, from Warren Zevon to Phil Spector and Herb Alpert, went to school here too. Dozens of well-known actors also attended class at Fairfax, including Carole Lombard, Mickey Rooney, Demi Moore, and Mila Kunis, to name only a few. There are professional athletes and politicians. The list goes on and on. The school has of course appeared on screen itself, notably in the pilot episode of *American Horror Story*.

School's out on Sundays, though, and the campus is covered in booths hawking their fabulous wares. There's amazing shopping to do, and people to watch doing it. You'll find a highly curated experience, where you can find clothing, art, vintage cameras, stereos, and so much more. If vintage isn't your thing, don't worry. There are booths with delicious food, plants, handmade crafts, and new products being beta tested before going to a larger market. The Melrose Trading Post is where you can see and be seen, and find those special unique items that cannot be found anywhere else.

Address 7850 Melrose Avenuc, Hollywood, CA 90046, www.melrosetradingpost.org |
Getting there Bus 10, 217, 218 to Melrose/Fairfax | Hours Sun 9am–5pm | Tip Kosher
News is a good old-fashioned newsstand that's been here for ages, and they sell actual paper
magazines and newspapers (370 N Fairfax Avenue, www.westernkosher.com).

65 Metro Station Art
Art to behold at Hollywood/Vine

For the entire decade of the 1990s, the late, great Chicano artist Gilbert "Magu" Luján, designed, planned, and executed the artwork for the Metro station at Hollywood and Vine. From the street level plaza all the way down to the subway platform, you'll experience his works, as you wander through a dreamy station that feels like a movie about an anthropomorphic train depot who wants to grow up to be a movie theater. There are two giant, vintage movie cameras as sentinels in the lobby and thousands of film reels lining the ceiling of the tunnel where trains rush in. Sprockets from film cells line the walls and doorways, and evocative artwork is tucked into every corner.

Working closely with architect Adolfo Miralles, Luján created the feel, based in part on the famous song, "Hooray for Hollywood," from the 1937 movie *Hollywood Hotel*. The design is a mashup of tributes to the film industry, complete with a gold-tiled nod to the yellow brick road from *The Wizard of Oz*, combined with Luján's distinctive style that has come to represent the Chicano art movement. In a nod to his own fascination with cars, riders rest throughout the station on sculptural benches in the shape of lowriders. More than 200 colorful, hand-glazed art tiles depicting themes from films are placed here and there, as well as some from Luján's own lexicon of Chicano imagery. The hand railing along the stairs even displays the musical notes from "Hooray for Hollywood."

Metro riders who are lucky enough to use this delightful station are left with an impression that is at once whimsical and nostalgic. It's pretty common to see riders pausing to study some detail in the station, rather than rushing through on their way to somewhere else. For those who love art, and for those who are wistful for the Golden Age of Hollywood, this train station itself is a destination worth visiting, thanks to the vision of Gilbert Luján.

Address Hollywood Boulevard & Vine Avenue, Hollywood, CA 90028, art.metro.net | Getting there Metro B to Hollywood/Vine (Red Line) | Hours Unrestricted | Tip Check out *Underground Girl* by Sheila Klein at the Hollywood/Highland Station (art.metro.net/artworks/underground-girl).

66 Miceli's Restaurant
A slice of Old Hollywood

Step through the doorway of the oldest pizzeria in Hollywood, and you're suddenly in the Golden Age again. When owner Frank Miceli greets you beneath thousands of hanging Chianti bottles, it's easy to imagine his father Carmen and his mother Sylvia at the grand opening in 1949. Carmen Miceli was a war hero with four Purple Heart medals, a Bronze Star, and a secret weapon: his Sicilian mother's Old-World Italian recipes. Is it any wonder that a steady stream of celebrities, including Marilyn Monroe, The Beatles, Ronald Reagan, Orson Welles, Frank Sinatra, and countless others, flowed through this place? Stars still flock here today – Julia Roberts, Jim Carrey, and Adam Sandler are all regulars.

History is literally embedded in this restaurant. Many of the booths and elaborate ornamental wall panels came from the legendary Pig n' Whistle when it closed. You can still see the pig that was beautifully carved into the back panel of some of the wooden booths in 1927.

With its checkered tablecloths and stained-glass windows, Miceli's still looks exactly like it did on the day that Lucille Ball learned how to toss a pizza here for an episode of *I Love Lucy*. It was just the same when Linda Hamilton as her character Sarah Connor was chased into the upstairs bar for a scene in *The Terminator*. Ask Frank to tell you about John F. Kennedy or Elizabeth Taylor coming in for a meal, and you may find that you're sitting in the very same booth where they enjoyed their meatballs.

If you're lucky, you'll find something else from the old days within these storied walls. Legend has it that the ghost of Toni Colavecchi Hines, a favorite Miceli's waitress, haunts this place. If you hear the crash of a glass falling off a table, or a door suddenly slamming shut, go pay your respects to Toni's stained-glass memorial portrait that hangs in the corner of her old section, and she'll settle down.

Address 1646 N Las Palmas Avenue, Hollywood, CA 90028, +1 (323) 466-3438,
www.micelis.restaurant | Getting there Metro B to Hollywood/Highland (Red Line) |
Hours Daily 11:30am–9pm | Tip After your pizza, stroll around the corner to the
Supply Sergeant, an amazing military surplus store that will meet all of your survivalist
needs (6664 Hollywood Boulevard, www.thesupplysergeant.com).

67__Monastery of Angels
Baking away our sins

Everyone knows that Hollywood has a lurid and often dark history filled with seamy tales of sex, drugs, and movie star mayhem. Less well known is the fact that there's a rich and diverse religious life here as well. One of the most delightful – and delicious – examples is the Monastery of Angels Convent.

The convent was founded in 1924 by Mother Mary of the Eucharist and four other nuns from the holiest of holy places: Newark, New Jersey. They were originally housed in downtown Los Angeles, but before too long, they had set up shop in the Giroux family mansion in Hollywood. The original group have all passed on, but the mansion is still the home to this order of cloistered Dominican nuns.

While these dedicated sisters have largely withdrawn from the world through their religious life, thankfully they have not forsworn what they call "Monastery goodies." Chocolates and peanut brittle stream from their bakery like benedictions, and the pumpkin bread tastes like it was blessed in heaven itself.

The grounds are open to visitors, so take a stroll through the lovely gardens and enjoy the peace and quiet. If you're so moved, you can pray alongside the residents in the Chapel of Perpetual Adoration, where, as the name suggests, at least one sister is always praying, through the day and night. Then on to the gift shop, where, if you can tear yourself away from the case full of mouthwatering candies, breads, and cakes, you'll find all of the religious books, cards, and candles you'd expect, but also original paintings, crafts, and other charming doodads handmade by the residents.

Visiting the Monastery of Angels Convent is a pleasant diversion from both the glitz and the grime of Hollywood. Whether you're seeking a contemplative break from the secular world, or you just have a sweet tooth, you'll leave this place with your spirit and your palate thoroughly satisfied.

Address 1977 Carmen Avenue, Hollywood, CA 90068, +1 (323) 466-2186, www.monasteryoftheangels.org, goodies@monasteryoftheangels.org | **Getting there** Bus DASH Beachwood Canyon, DASH Hollywood to Franklin/Vista Del Mar | **Hours** Daily 6am – 5pm, call for gift shop hours | **Tip** For another interesting religious destination, the Krotona temple, original home of the Theosophical movement, is a short walk from the monastery (2130 Vista Del Mar Avenue).

68 Morrison Hotel Gallery

Photo heaven for music lovers

In 1970, the iconic rock band The Doors went walking around downtown Los Angeles with legendary rock photographer Henry Diltz looking for a cool place to take some pictures for their new album. They found a dive bar, now long gone, called the Hard Rock Café, where they shot the back cover – and inspired the global Hard Rock Café franchise.

For the front cover image, they went to a location that Ray Manzarek, the band's keyboard player, had found on South Hope Street downtown. It was a gritty hotel with the same name as the Doors' lead singer, and the band snuck in to take the shot that wound up on the front cover of the famous Doors album: *Morrison Hotel*.

The Morrison Hotel still exists, and it remains a somewhat gritty downtown hotel. But the *Morrison Hotel* album and the photograph from its cover are revered as icons of rock and roll. So it's appropriate that one of the greatest curations of fine-art rock and roll photography is housed at the Morrison Hotel Gallery. It's not a coincidence. One of the owners of the gallery is the renowned photographer from that shoot all those decades ago, Henry Diltz.

Diltz is responsible for some of the most recognizable and influential music photos of all time, but his famous pictures are just the tip of the iceberg at the Morrison Hotel Gallery. Thousands of photographs, captured by hundreds of the world's top photographers, are available for purchase at the gallery, which is located in the lobby of the swanky Sunset Marquis Hotel in West Hollywood.

Bands and artists spanning many decades of time and across musical genres are represented, from ABBA to ZZ Top, and everything in between, including the Morrison Hotel cover shot for which the gallery is named. A pilgrimage to the Morrison Hotel Gallery is an absolute must for collectors of music photography. When you visit, you might just be inspired to kickstart a collection of your own.

Address 1200 Alta Loma Road, West Hollywood, CA 90069, +1 (310) 881-6025, www.morrisonhotelgallery.com | Getting there Bus 16, 105 to Holloway/La Cienega | Hours Mon–Sat 11am–6pm, Sun noon–5pm | Tip Now that you've looked at the photos, go see a rock show for yourself at the world-famous Whisky a Go-Go just down the street (8901 W Sunset Boulevard, www.whiskyagogo.com).

69 Muhammad Ali's Star

Look up to see this star

Sitting atop the list of all-time best sports heroes is "The Greatest," the one and only Muhammad Ali. Ali rocketed to stardom after winning the gold medal in boxing's light heavyweight division at the 1960 Summer Olympic Games in Rome, and he went on to become the heavyweight champion of the world three different times. He is revered as one of the greatest athletes ever. His activism and philanthropy also contribute to his stature among the most celebrated Americans in history.

But don't look for this star embedded in the sidewalk on Hollywood's legendary Walk of Fame. Muhammad Ali's star can instead be found mounted on the outer wall of the Dolby Theater. Why is this important star, out of more than 2,700, the only one that is not underfoot? The answer lies in the boxer's name and deep Muslim faith. "I bear the name of our beloved prophet Mohammad, and it is impossible that I allow people to trample over his name," Ali said of his star. In fact, he initially rejected the honor because of the conundrum of where it would be placed.

Due to the singularity of its vertical presentation and the underlying spiritual rationale, Ali's star has come to represent far more than simply an homage to a celebrity who was also a great fighter. In fact, Muslims from around the world come to visit the star and often feel moved not only by the memorial to an important public figure, but also by the meaning behind hanging the honor on the wall rather than placing it on the ground.

In a town that loves storytelling, it's the *story* of Ali's star and why it is presented so respectfully that really matters to those who visit it. So when you look up at his star, remember that Muhammad Ali wanted to be remembered "...As a man who never looked down on those who looked up to him ... who stood up for his beliefs ... who tried to unite all humankind through faith and love."

Address 6801 Hollywood Boulevard, Hollywood, CA 90028, +1 (323) 469-8311, www.walkoffame.com/muhammad-ali | Getting there Metro B to Hollywood/Highland (Red Line); bus 212, 217 to Hollywood/Highland | Hours Unrestricted | Tip While you're enjoying unusual Walk of Fame markers, look for the Apollo 11 astronaut crew markers on all four street corners at Hollywood and Vine (www.walkoffame.com/special-apollo-xi). But they aren't stars – they are moons!

70 The Mulholland Dam

Scary hidden masterpiece of engineering

It seems that even many locals have forgotten that there's a lovely lake shimmering right in the middle of Hollywood. It's a beautiful, picture-postcard scene, and it's truly a delight to walk or jog around the paved perimeter.

You'd think that locals would remember Lake Hollywood. After all, it has frequently appeared in the movies. In *Chinatown*, Hollis Mulwray is found dead on its shore, and in the 1974 disaster film *Earthquake*, the dam terrifyingly collapses and floods what's left of Los Angeles after a giant temblor. The real-life story of the lake and dam is almost as unnerving.

The Mulholland Dam was completed in 1924 and celebrated as a modern masterpiece of engineering. The majesty of towering white walls soaring heroically above the city, and the picturesque glassy waters (up to 2.5 billion horrifying gallons) all seemed to proclaim William Mulholland as the king of aqueduct engineers. But the honeymoon didn't last. A mere four years later, and only 25 miles away, the nearly identical St. Francis Dam failed spectacularly, flooding Santa Clara Valley and killing more than 430 people.

Panic ensued, and the future of the Mulholland Dam was seriously called into question. William Mulholland said the dam was safe, but that's what he had said about St. Francis too. With the specter of Hollywood being flooded, nobody was buying it this time. In order to make the lake and dam safer – and to provide a "psychological dam" to assuage concerns – the dam was literally *buried* under 330,000 cubic yards of earth and vegetation, where it still resides, mostly invisible. The largely unaware neighborhood below remains blissfully ignorant today.

Despite this precaution, Mulholland, previously thought to be impervious to complaint, was forced out of his powerful role at Power Works and Supply and died long before his legacy began to be restored.

Address 3160 Canyon Lake Drive, Hollywood, CA 90068, +1 (818) 243-1145, www.laparks.org/park/lake-hollywood | Getting there By car, drive to entrances at Lake Hollywood Drive, Weidlake Drive, or Tahoe Drive, then follow the signs to the dam. | Hours Daily dawn – dusk | Tip After walking around the lake, enjoy a picnic in Lake Hollywood Park with one of the best views of the iconic Hollywood Sign.

71 Museum of Antique Cinema Cameras

Movie history behind the scenes

From the 1940s through the 1960s, Paramount Pictures won more than 70 Oscars, including Best Picture for *My Fair Lady* and *The Godfather*. The type of camera responsible for filming every single one of them was the mighty Mitchell BNC, or "Blimped Newsreel Camera." It is no flimsy handheld camera. This big beast required at least two strong people to heave it onto a tripod. A man named Greg Toland rented one of these tanks to shoot a little movie back in 1941, and it is now on display in one of the coolest museums in Hollywood. The movie? Just a little something called *Citizen Kane*. The museum? It's the rather unheralded but totally spectacular antique cinema camera collection at the American Society of Cinematographers (ASC).

Founded in 1919, the ASC was created to advance the art and science of cinematography. The organization moved into this Mission Revival home, which was then a private residence, in 1936. It wasn't just any private residence, either. This was once the home of Conway Tearle, a major movie star in the Silent Era, who was featured in nearly 100 films and was once the highest paid actor in Hollywood.

The museum and library, including a remarkable collection of movie cameras, is the only one of its kind in the world. There are cameras here dating back to the 19th century, and it's incredible to see up close the evolution of camera technology over the course of a century. Some of these early contraptions make it seem implausible that movies were ever made at all.

Open to the public, this museum is a must for cinephiles, camera lovers, and history buffs alike. Like the camera used by Greg Toland, the machines on display were used by some of the world's greatest cinematographers to film many of the most popular and important films ever produced.

Address 1782 N Orange Drive, Hollywood, CA 90028, +1 (323) 969-4333, www.theasc.com | Getting there Metro B to Hollywood/Highland (Red Line) | Hours Tours by appointment only | Tip If you're into old cameras, you may want to check out Freestyle Photo, one of the last remaining places that support film photography (5401 Sunset Boulevard, www.freestylephoto.biz).

72 __Musso & Frank Grill

Most iconic martini in Hollywood

"James Bond had it all wrong," according to Andrea Scuto, the general manager of the Musso & Frank Grill. "Never shake the martini." He should know. The martini at Hollywood's oldest restaurant is the stuff of legends, and has been enjoyed by some of the world's most beloved movie stars, authors, politicians, and many others. Whether you select gin or vodka as your base alcohol, the martini will be stirred carefully about a dozen times by one of Musso's world-class bartenders to preserve the texture of the alcohol and to avoid bruising the aromatics. There won't be any vermouth – just two olives, Spanish of course, cured and brined in-house with herbs and peppers. Your drink is served in a tiny, two-and-a-half-ounce glass to ensure that it stays cold. It comes with a sidecar refill in a bucket of crushed ice. The result is absolutely perfect and has been just that way for over 100 years.

Since 1919, the classic beverage has been served at this equally classic restaurant. The menu hasn't changed, and even some of the staff have been working here for decades. Charlie Chaplin was a regular, and so were Greta Garbo and Humphrey Bogart. In every era, Musso's has been the go-to place for A-listers to satiate their palates with a perfectly prepared steak and to wet their whistles with a sturdy cocktail or two. Writers John Steinbeck, Kurt Vonnegut, and Dorothy Parker found a home here, along with Groucho Marx, Elizabeth Taylor, and dozens of other luminaries. The martini that you sip here has been served to thousands of sophisticated guests over the decades, many of whom were icons themselves.

Yes, time marches on, but some things are better left unchanged. Musso & Frank is a testament to the power of tradition. Like the martini itself, your emotions and your taste buds will be stirred, and not shaken, when you lift this classic to your lips.

Address 6667 Hollywood Boulevard, Hollywood, CA 90028, +1 (323) 467-7788, www.mussoandfrank.com | Getting there Metro B to Hollywood/Highland (Red Line); bus 217 to Hollywood/Las Palmas | Hours Tue–Sat 5–11pm, Sun 4–10pm | Tip When there's no room at the bar, another iconic watering hole is right around the corner. Boardner's has been satiating Hollywood since 1942 (1652 N Cherokee Avenue, www.boardners.com).

73 Native Voices

Native American theater at the Autry Museum

At the edge of Griffith Park, tucked into the esteemed Autry Museum of the American West, is a charming little theater. It's the typical kind of venue for a museum, one where you'd expect to see a busload of schoolchildren marching in to "enjoy" an educational presentation of some kind. But in truth, this quaint auditorium is far more special. This is the home to the only professional theatre company in the country dedicated exclusively to developing and producing new works by Indigenous writers and performers.

Native Voices was co-founded in 1994 by actors Randy Reinholtz, a member of the Choctaw Nation, and his partner, Jean Bruce Scott. As young actors, the couple both began their careers on the soap opera *Days of Our Lives*. They have built Native Voices together, first as the Autry's resident theatre company, and then building it into the prestigious and important creative institution that it is today for the underserved Indigenous community. Many productions that began at Native Voices have gone on to larger companies around the country, including the Oregon Shakespeare Festival, The Public Theatre in New York, and the La Jolla Playhouse.

A rich part of many Native American cultures are the stories and rituals that have traditionally been expressed through dance, music, and other theatrical forms. Native Voices is one of many groups that are bringing the stories and perspectives of Indigenous people onto the stage and into the canon of modern theatrical works.

So sure, schoolkids do rumble into the hall for a variety of productions at the Autry Museum. But if it's a Native Voices show, you can rest assured that those kids will be encountering – and enjoying – a play that is grounded in the vision and authenticity of storytelling from an Indigenous perspective that is at the core of what this groundbreaking theatre company is all about.

Address 4700 Western Heritage Way, Hollywood, CA 90027, +1 (323) 667-2000, www.theautry.org/native-voices-at-the-autry, communications@theautry.org | Getting there Bus 96 to Autry National Center | Hours See website for performance and event schedule | Tip The Tongva people lived in the Los Angeles Basin for centuries, and there are many historic and/or sacred places, including Tongva Peak (Beaudry Loop Trail, entrance near 1300 Beaudry Boulevard).

74_New Beverly Cinema
Tarantino's film-only theater

The New Beverly Cinema isn't your average theater by any stretch of the imagination. How many other movie houses used to be a candy store, a Jewish community center, and a porno theater? No, not all at the same time (that's a bit too much, even for Hollywood). It started as a candy store in 1929, and became each of those other things in the subsequent decades, finally moving from adult films to more mainstream movies in 1978. The owner then was local legend Sherman Torgan, who loved movies and wanted to share them with the world. He'd show double features of everything from arthouse movies to old classics and foreign films, and some aficionados thought of his curated offerings as a kind of film school. One such audience member was Quentin Tarantino.

When Tarantino began to find success in the movie industry as a film director, he became a benefactor of the theater, and in 2007, he became its owner and head programmer. He doubled down on the Torgan way of showing movies: a double feature (sometimes a triple for special occasions) of carefully curated films, only shown on film, no digital. "As long as I'm alive," said Tarantino, "and as long as I'm rich, the New Bev will be showing double features in 35mm."

It's an audacious approach, but that suits Tarantino's personality and commitment to cinema. He programs much of the content himself, some of it from his own large collection of films. You'll see independent premieres; mini festivals representing a director, style, or country of origin; and of course, the long-running "Grindhouse Tuesdays," celebrating that genre.

So don't come to the New Beverly Cinema to see the latest action franchise blockbuster, or a digital print of any kind. Do come to be with film lovers, cinephiles, and the occasional Oscar-winning director to enjoy films as they were meant to be seen: in film and on the silver screen.

Address 7165 Beverly Boulevard, Hollywood, CA 90036, +1 (323) 938-4038, www.thenewbev.com |
Getting there Bus 14, 37, 212 bus to Beverly/La Brea | Hours See website for schedule |
Tip Get outfitted for that old movie you're going to see by stopping in at a great vintage
clothing store, Jet Rag (825 N La Brea Avenue, www.facebook.com/JetRagClothing).

75 __ The Old Zoo
The ruins of Griffith Park

This story sounds like a plot from a bad Hollywood movie. The city decides to build a zoo in the biggest park in town, but the funding falls through. The oddball entrepreneur for whom the park is named has a business partner, a "naturalist" with the subtle name of Dr. Charles Sketchley, who had run a successful ostrich farm. Sketchley had abandoned an assortment of animals when he moved his ostriches out of town, and voila: a zoo is born! What could possibly go wrong?

It's no movie, but it's bad, alright. With a whopping budget of $2,000 dollars squeezed out of the city council and a paltry 15 animals including Sketchley's, the Griffith Park Zoo limped into existence in 1912. Over the next decade, the zoo grew. Two other local zoos went out of business as World War I raged overseas, and their frail inhabitants wound up in Griffith Park. But problems with unsanitary enclosures and unethical treatment of the animals led to severe criticism, fines, and derision. By the mid-1920s, the zoo was on the brink of closure.

Despite valiant attempts, including an infusion of WPA money in the 1930s, the zoo continued to struggle. It was a fiasco. Animals died, weird accidents and bizarre incidents were run of the mill, and the complaints about the zoo grew louder. The Griffith Park Zoo was finally shut down in the 1960s, but the ruins still stand today.

The steel cages and fake stone enclosures make a lousy place to live, but they're a really great weird picnic spot. They are also regularly used for television and film shoots (like the bear scene from *Anchorman*) and birthday parties. In the summertime, there are free Shakespeare productions and concerts. It's an easy hike around the ruins of the old zoo, where you can still see the cages, caves and enclosures that housed unhappy creatures all those years ago, when Dr. Sketchley's abandoned animals moved in.

Address 4801 Griffith Park Drive, Hollywood, CA 90027, +1 (323) 913-4688, www.alltrails.com/trail/us/california/griffith-park-old-zoo-loop | Getting there By car, enter Griffith Park from Riverside Drive, which turns into Crystal Springs Road, left onto Griffith Park Drive. | Hours Daily 5:30am–10pm | Tip The Los Angeles Zoo is an actual working zoo just down the street, and it's world class (5333 Zoo Drive, www.lazoo.org).

76 The ONE Gallery

Best place to see queer art

The ONE Archives Foundation is the oldest active LGBTQIA+ organization in the United States. It was started in 1952 to support the launch of *ONE* magazine, which would become the first widely distributed magazine for the LGBTQIA+ community. The ONE Institute, the educational wing of the foundation, came along shortly thereafter, offering classes and seminars, and eventually even issuing advanced degrees.

During those formative years, one of the key participants in all of the ONE activities was a man named Jim Kepner. Kepner had been collecting all kinds of materials related to LGBTQIA+ topics and people since the 1940s. His personal library grew so large over the years that in 1971, he named it the Western Gay Archives, at which point it instantly became known as an important resource in the community. The sizable collection was beginning to take over his home and needed to be relocated, and so it moved to a storefront on Hudson Avenue in Hollywood, with a fresh new name: The National Gay Archives. It kept on growing, and it was relocated in 1988 to Robertson Boulevard and renamed again, this time as the International Gay & Lesbian Archives, or IGLA.

In 1994, the IGLA collection became part of the ONE Institute and moved to the University of Southern California, where it remains. It's the largest collection of LGBTQIA+ materials in the world.

Such a collection needs a way to be seen, which means there's a need for exhibitions. And those exhibitions take place at the ONE Gallery, which is located at the former IGLA site on Robertson. This venue showcases the work of LGBTQIA+ artists, drawing not only from the archives, but from all manner of currently working artists. It's an important part of the legacy of the ONE Archives Foundation, celebrating the vision and voice of artists in the community, and it's one of the best places anywhere to see art.

Address 626 N Robertson Boulevard, West Hollywood, CA 90069, +1 (323) 968-0410, www.onearchives.org | Getting there Bus 10, 16, 48 to San Vicente/Melrose | Hours See website for exhibitions | Tip West Hollywood Park, just up the street, is home to *Parallel Perpendicular*, a public art piece by Phillip K. Smith III (647 N San Vicente Boulevard, www.publicartinpublicplaces.info).

77 — Opal Tattoo

Female-owned tattoo sanctuary

If you're looking for a place to get a pin-up girl tattooed on your bicep, or a picture of your favorite superhero, corporate logo, or rockstar emblazoned on your chest, then you'd probably be better off looking elsewhere. Zara Solava isn't very interested in reproducing that kind of boilerplate art. At Opal Tattoo, Solava's Hollywood studio, making a tattoo is a far more personal process than simply leafing through a book of popular designs.

Solava wants to get to know each client a little bit before putting one of her beautiful, fine-line designs on their bodies. She knows it's a big decision, and she doesn't take the responsibility lightly. It's part of her commitment to making the process "as easy and painless as possible," she says. The whole studio embodies that feeling of warmth and welcoming. Not only will you get the necessary support and care in designing your tattoo and putting it on your body, but you can also buy most of the art on the walls as well, all made by local artists. The little shop at the studio even sells things like baby clothes, candles, and ceramics.

While everyone is welcome, it shouldn't be too surprising to learn that around 80% of Solava's clients are women. After all, three-quarters of all tattoo artists are men. "When you walk into most tattoo shops, it's pretty much all dudes," says Solava, "and it's very intimidating. My shop is beautiful and light and a safe place for anyone. There's no pressure." Sometimes people walk in to buy a candle and ask about getting a massage, thinking it's a wellness spa.

It's important to Solava that she brings her special brand of tattoo parlor to this neighborhood in Hollywood. She was born and raised here, and she played t-ball right down the street when she was a kid. If you're looking for a comfortable place for a unique piece of tattoo art from a talented local artist, look no further than Opal Tattoo.

Address 7466 Beverly Boulevard, Suite 101, Hollywood, CA 90036, +1 (323) 433-4900, www.opaltattooink.com | Getting there Bus 14, 37 to Beverly/Gardner | Hours Daily 11am–6pm | Tip Erewhon is a very fancy natural foods supermarket, where you can find all the most handcrafted and bespoke healthy stuff you may need (7660 Beverly Boulevard, www.erewhonmarket.com).

78_The Pacific Design Center
Massive creativity inside the Blue Whale

The behemoth blue whale is the largest animal ever known to exist. And one look at the massive blue building that houses the Pacific Design Center explains why it was nicknamed after the huge mammal.

The "Blue Whale" is big – 1.6-*million*-square-feet kind of big. It's large enough to house almost 100 luxury showrooms filled with more than 2,000 of the most cutting-edge brands in interior design and architecture, and still leave room for meeting rooms for 10 to 2,500 people, galas (Elton John's famous annual Oscar party is held here), and film shoots, and that's not all. There's a 300-seat movie theater inside, and a terrace that can handle a reception for 1,200 revelers without feeling crowded. That's not even including the two restaurants, the enormous lobby, an atrium, and other stunning, rentable venue spaces to be found in the 14-acre campus. It's really quite large.

The design center itself is not all blue – the other buildings are green and red. But the blue building is the one actually known as the Blue Whale. It's "only" 750,000 square feet in size. The showrooms and shops inside are at the leading edge of interior design, and a great place to learn about current trends in design of all kinds, and of course, shop to your heart's content. There's also a red building and a green one, each more than 400,000 square feet, where countless firms in the fields of art, fashion, architecture, and technology, rent creative office space.

Even without considering the impressive spaces inside, where all the exhibitions and events are held, these buildings themselves are a sight to behold. They comprise an enormous, angular, and colorful work of art designed by Cesar Pelli that makes the surrounding neighborhood seem to shrink to the size of a helpless school of krill, content with its fate to be gobbled up by the beautiful and truly gigantic Blue Whale.

Address 8687 Melrose Avenue, West Hollywood, CA 90069, +1 (310) 657-0800, www.pacificdesigncenter.com | Getting there Bus 10, 16, 48 to San Vicente/Melrose | Hours Mon–Fri 9am–5pm | Tip Speaking of design, the late, great punk fashion icon Vivienne Westwood's store is nearby (8320 Melrose Avenue, www.viviennewestwood.com).

79_The Pagoda
Drinks at the oldest structure in California

High on a hilltop in Hollywood, with a majestic view of the city, sits a Japanese-*ish* castle. Yamashiro, which translates as "mountain palace," was completed in 1914, and many of the materials did indeed come from Japan. The design, however, commissioned by German brothers Adolph and Eugene Bernheimer, is American. They were avid collectors of Asian artifacts and wanted a place where they could live comfortably and display their extensive collection.

The architecture and décor, however, has been called "a caricature," replete with Chinese, Japanese, and other Asian influences and attributes. And that's only one reason that controversy about Yamashiro has bubbled up over the last century. There was vandalism and violence during the internment of Japanese Americans during World War II, as well as complaints and discontent over the years about the "Asian-Fusion" design, with accusations of cultural appropriation.

There is one piece of the Yamashiro campus that is undeniably authentic, though. The 600-year-old Japanese pagoda that is the centerpiece of the Yama Shisha Hookah Lounge, at the swimming pool just below the restaurant, was brought here from Kyoto, Japan in 1914. It's the oldest structure in all of California. The views from here are stunning, and the quiet beauty of the lounge and environs make this one of the most romantic locations in Hollywood and beyond.

The restaurant itself is a Hollywood fixture, and it unironically serves "Asian-Fusion" food that is extremely delicious. It's always packed to the rafters with eager diners, and the Hookah Lounge can be pretty busy as well, so make a reservation. This is a date night destination at the top of Hollywood, where you can see a gorgeous sunset or just watch the twinkling lights of Tinseltown below. And nowhere else in California can you smoke a hookah beside an ancient structure that found itself somehow transported to this spot.

Address 1999 N Sycamore Avenue, Hollywood, CA 90068, +1 (323) 466-5125, www.yamashirohollywood.com, reception@yamashirohollywood.com | Getting there By car, drive north on N Sycamore Avenue from Franklin Avenue | Hours Daily 5–11pm by reservation | Tip In the wonderful nearby Whitley Heights neighborhood you'll find the lovely Villa Vallombrosa, which has been called "the most romantic house in Hollywood." Maybe that's why Leonard Bernstein once lived there (2074 Watsonia Terrace).

80 Pause Studio
The future of relaxation

It looks and feels like something from a science fiction movie. There's a blue light glowing, and calm music gently wafts through the air. You hear a soothing voice giving you instructions, so you take a few meditative breaths, put in your earplugs, and gently lower yourself into the warm fluid of the orb.

Yes, the orb. The Float Orb, to be more precise. At over eight feet long and nearly six feet wide, it's large enough for almost anyone to float freely in this tub filled with saltwater. The sense of weightlessness and sensory deprivation you'll feel is what gives the experience its relaxing and surreal quality. And there are apparently many health benefits to giving your body 45 minutes to relieve itself of the burden of carrying you around every single day. Some fans of the experience say that it feels like you're drifting in outer space, free from earthly anxieties and responsibilities.

Floating is, of course, only one of the beneficial options on the decadent menu of wellness offerings at Pause Studio, which has become known as one of the best places in town for a wide variety of spa treatments. They offer the most cutting-edge technology, like a cryogenic chamber that will freeze you – in a good way – for three minutes at -200 degrees Fahrenheit. You can also go back and forth from a cold plunge to a hot sauna, known as contrast therapy, which is intended to help heal inflammation and make you sleep better, among other benefits. The array of weird and wonderful treatments don't end there. You can have an intravenous infusion of vitamins, regenerate cells with LED lights, or get compression therapy too.

Hollywood can feel like a high-octane, exciting place to be, fun and full of adventure. Every once in a while, it might be good to just pause. A visit to Pause Studio is a refreshing and futuristic way to destress. It's all science, but not fiction.

Address 937 N Sycamore Avenue, Hollywood, CA 90038, +1 (323) 565-9381, www.pausestudio.com | Getting there Bus 212 to La Brea/Willoughby | Hours Daily 8:30am–10pm | Tip Your pets need the spa experience as well so take them to Collar & Comb (7813 W Sunset Boulevard, www.collarandcomb.dog).

81 Philosophical Research Society Library

A bibliophile's mystical paradise

Born in 1901, Manly P. Hall spent his life as a spiritual seeker. His obsession with all things mystical, occult, and metaphysical led to a spectacular collection of books from around the world, detailing the sacred and outlandish traditions. Hall's own book, a compendium of wisdom called *The Secret Teachings of All Ages*, became an important encyclopedia of esoterica to the degree that Elvis Presley was reputed to have been so inspired that he gave copies of it to his bandmates and everyone else in his sphere.

Hall's pedigree as a great thinker, his reputation as a psychic, and his somewhat odd presence in Hollywood society led to friendships with such disparate figures as Bela Lugosi, whose wedding he officiated, to John Denver, a fellow seeker. Hall "accidentally" became the leader of a church, stating "...it was one of those circumstances of fortune that you do not question...." He also wrote screenplays, pamphlets, and treatises, becoming Hollywood's foremost mystical guru, a title he rejected.

Hall founded the Philosophical Research Society (PRS) in 1934, which still holds his impressive collection of books, pamphlets, and ephemera. The stated goal was to help "thoughtful persons to live more graciously and constructively in a confused and troubled world...." The library, open to the public, is an impressive repository of arcana and mysticism. It's been designated a cultural site, in part due to the beautiful architecture of Robert Stacy-Judd.

In 1985, Hall officiated the wedding of the legendary and cantankerous Charles Bukowski in the PRS library. Although he died five years later, the legacy of Manly P. Hall lives on here. Classes, lectures, art exhibitions, and over 50,000 volumes of weird and/or soulful books to peruse make this place an absolute must.

Address 3910 Los Feliz Boulevard, Hollywood, CA 90027, +1 (323) 663-2167, www.prs.org/ library.html, info@prs.org | Getting there By car, take Los Feliz Boulevard to Griffith Park Boulevard | Hours Fri noon–6pm open to the public, Tue–Thu noon–6pm by appointment | Tip The Los Angeles River is just to the East, where you can ride your bike, run or walk down the well maintained path, and even take a kayak onto the river in some places (https://lariverkayaksafari.org).

82 Pink's Hot Dogs

Celebrity weenie roast

In 1939, Betty Pink borrowed 50 dollars from her mother to buy a hot dog cart. That was a lot of money back then, and the chili dogs that Betty made were only going to sell for 10 cents each. They knew they were taking a gamble, but Betty and her husband Paul took the plunge and began hocking hot dogs on the corner of Melrose and La Brea. By 1946, they had raised the price of their wieners to 25 cents. They managed to scrape together enough money to buy the little piece of land where they'd been parking their cart. A small bank loan put a roof overhead and a few tables inside, and it's been a Hollywood institution ever since.

The custom-made dogs are incredibly delicious and creative, and that's certainly part of why people are willing to stand in long lines to risk a mustard stain from Pink's. But there are other reasons too. For one thing, celebrities seem to be absolutely wild about this place. Even beyond the folks whose names and regular orders are on the menu, like Martha Stewart or Drew Barrymore, Pink's has always been a great place to see famous faces. Maybe they just love the food. Legend has it that Orson Welles once ate 18 Pink's dogs in one sitting. Whatever the reasons, celebrity sightings are common here, and the wall of fame inside proves it. In a particularly dramatic moment, Brad Pitt even got abducted here once. It turned out to be a prank for the TV show *Jackass*, but it certainly got diners riled up.

Pink's isn't just popular with stars – it has a pretty impressive resume all on its own. This restaurant has made a lot of appearances in films, including hits like *Mulholland Drive* and *The Muppets*. There have also been television appearances on *Hell's Kitchen*, *Entourage*, and many others. It's open until 2am on the weekends, so come for a bite at the end of your night, and who knows? You may be dining with the Hollywood elite.

Address 709 N La Brea Avenue, Hollywood, CA 90038, +1 (323) 931-4223, www.pinkshollywood.com | Getting there Bus 10, 48, 212 to La Brea/Melrose | Hours Sun–Thu 9:30am–midnight, Fri & Sat 9:30–2am | Tip For a tasty dessert after your dog, head over to Milk Bar, where you can buy delicious yums, or take a class and learn how to make them yourself (7150 Melrose Avenue, www.milkbarstore.com).

83 — The Pleasure Chest
Battery empowered

If you were listening carefully, you heard about The Pleasure Chest in the 1978 Queen song, "Let Me Entertain You." Iconic frontman Freddie Mercury was never shy about sex and sexuality in his songs, so the lyric, "If you want to see some action / We got nothing but the best / The S&M attraction / We got The Pleasure Chest," was simply an unabashed celebration of pleasure – and a full-throated endorsement of one of the best sex shops ever.

The Pleasure Chest initially opened in New York's West Village in 1971. It was the very first store of its kind to buck the tradition of having darkened or covered windows and a sense of shame for shoppers. The sex-positive, inclusive ethic of the place made it an essential part of the sexual liberation movement of the 1970s and also cemented its reputation with people of all genders and orientations. No matter who you were, they wanted to help make your sex life better, and, like Freddie Mercury, they weren't going to be shy about it.

The West Hollywood location is bright and welcoming, with knowledgeable and kind staff, who help create an environment where "everyone has a fundamental right to pursue sexual fulfillment." In pursuit of that dream, The Pleasure Chest doesn't just sell awesome toys, but also focuses on education with their PleasurEd program, which includes workshops about sexual health and tutorials that'll teach you how to do all kinds of sexy stuff. Free classes and groups are available both online and at the store, and they offer a library of informative blog posts about everything your filthy mind can dream up.

Whether it's your first time in an adult store or you're a long-time customer, it's easy to enjoy your shopping experience at The Pleasure Chest (and then again and again when you get home). Join the likes of Queen Latifah, the Kardashians, Gwyneth Paltrow, and many other celebs who love coming here.

Address 7733 Santa Monica Boulevard, West Hollywood, CA 90046, +1 (323) 650-1022, www.thepleasurechest.com | Getting there Bus 4 to Santa Monica/Spaulding | Hours Sun–Wed noon–10pm, Thu–Sat noon–midnight | Tip If you're in the mood for adult shopping, stock up on erotica at Circus of Books (8230 Santa Monica Boulevard, www.circusofbooks.com).

84 The Record Parlour
Mecca of pre-digital entertainment

"Yes, kids, the legends are true. Way back in the olden days before the internet, when dinosaurs roamed the Earth, there was actually a way of listening to music on big discs made out of plastic…"

Ha. In reality, there's no need for waxing nostalgic or lectures from your grandparents because vinyl isn't just for the old folks anymore. Recording artists are back in the business of releasing vinyl again, so it's all the rage once more. Not that The Record Parlour shies away from the old-school feel. They have an impressive collection of vintage records to browse – there are more than 20,000 in the shop at any given time, and more than 250,000 in their warehouse! They've been called "An emporium of 20th century entertainment," and for good reason. There are a large assortment of cassettes, eight tracks, and other forms of analog recordings as well at this little Hollywood gem of a music store.

You'll find every kind of music, from priceless rarities to boxes and boxes of inexpensive but delightful, well-loved LPs. You can buy old video games, turntables, memorabilia, or even a fully restored vintage jukebox here. There are even antique radios, guitar amplifiers, speakers, and audio gear of all kinds. If you have any of that kind of equipment, or maybe some boxes of old albums collecting dust in the attic or a storage space, this wonderful place is always looking for quality stuff to buy.

Keep your ear to the ground by following them on social media, because there are occasional events featuring a performance by an artist or a DJ. Or just bring Grandma and Grandpa down to the store to reminisce about the good old days, but know that you'll be rubbing shoulders with all the music loving youngsters too. Professional DJs and audiophiles rejoice. The Record Parlour will become your new favorite place, even if you're only a casual listener.

Address 6408 Selma Avenue, Hollywood, CA 90028, +1 (323) 464-7757, www.facebook.com/therecordparlour, guest@therecordparlour.com | Getting there Bus 210, DASH Beachwood Canyon, DASH Hollywood to Selma/Vine | Hours Mon–Sat 10:30am–11:30pm, Sun 10am–10pm | Tip Los Angeles Contemporary Exhibitions, or LACE, is just down the street and always has great exhibitions (6522 Hollywood Boulevard, www.welcometolace.org).

85 Redd Foxx Walk of Fame

Poo Poo Man

The office building at 933 North La Brea occupies the plot of land where the offices of Redd Foxx Productions once stood. Redd Foxx is the legendary comedian who played Fred Sanford on the much beloved 1970s sitcom *Sanford and Son.* Although Foxx and most of the cast members of the show are no longer with us, and the building that formerly housed his company has been replaced, there's still a reason to visit this site: The Redd Foxx Walk of Fame.

The resemblance to the far better-known Hollywood Walk of Fame is slight. They're both on the sidewalk. They both bear the names of important people in the entertainment industry. But while the Hollywood Walk of Fame has thousands of beautiful handcrafted terrazzo and brass markers, with the letters of entertainment luminaries lovingly etched into them, the Redd Foxx version has mostly the names of people from *Sanford and Son* carved somewhat less elegantly into the cement sidewalk.

Wanda LaPage is there, the actress who played Aunt Esther on the show. Leroy Daniels & Ernest 'Skillet' Mayhand are there as well, the memorable comedy duo who appeared for two seasons as Fred's boisterous friends from the pool hall and the poker game. It's notable that the names in the sidewalk here are of mostly Black entertainers who were on a mostly Black television show. They aren't on the more famous Hollywood sidewalk, and while there are certainly many factors that contribute to that fact, it's likely that Redd Foxx and others were aware of these disparities.

One peculiar square looks as though it was put into the cement long after the sidewalk had dried. It's Poo Poo Man, also known as Gene Anderson, a musician who was a member of Parliament/Funkadelic. He doesn't seem to have appeared on *Sanford and Son*, but his distinctive moniker is here on the Redd Foxx Walk of Fame.

Address 933 N La Brea Avenue, Hollywood, CA 90038 | Getting there Bus 212 to La Brea/
Willoughby | Hours Unrestricted | Tip Mr. T is around the block, and offers a delicious take
on contemporary French cuisine (953 N Sycamore Avenue, www.mrtrestaurants.com).

86 Rock Town

Hollywood's punk boutique

There was a time when big hair and tight pants were ubiquitous on the streets of Hollywood. Clubs like Gazzarri's, Whisky a Go Go, and the Starwood were packed every night with rockers, headbanging to the hottest bands and adorned in the finery of leather, chains, corsets, and concert t-shirts. After hours at the Rainbow Bar and Grill or the Key Club, luminaries from John Lennon and Elvis Presley to hair bands like Ratt, Poison, and Mötley Crüe would hold court. The Sunset Strip was alive with heavy metal, punk, and rock 'n' roll, and crowds of band members, groupies, and wannabes spilled out of the throbbing clubs and swarmed the streets of Tinseltown.

Many of the clubs are gone now, consigned to the ashes of history but still burning hot in the memories of old rockers – undoubtedly, there are grandparents out there telling stories about rock royalty. Most of the classic bands have moved on to greener pastures, but hard rock is still an important part of the culture. Loud music pulses nightly from the Whisky and other boom rooms in Hollywood, and crowds of devoted fans are there, decked out to rock out. Distinct from the stereotypical aspiring actors or screenwriters, black-clad, tattooed rockers still abound, and there's something undeniably sexy and cool about this crowd. Rock Town is where they get the hot and gritty look.

It seems like it's been here forever on Hollywood Boulevard, and it's still the best place for enormous heavy metal shoes, or any punk gear, jackets, pins, buttons – you name it. If you're looking for Goth or industrial clothes and gear, or just concert shirts or posters for old-school rock bands, you'll find everything you need at Rock Town. The staff is friendly and helpful, the prices are good, and it's just a fun place to browse and check out the timeless vibe of Hollywood, where rock 'n' roll still rules.

Address 6709 Hollywood Boulevard, Hollywood, CA 90028, +1 (323) 462-7558,
www.rocktownhollywood.com, rocktownhollywood@gmail.com | Getting there Metro B
to Hollywood/Highland (Red Line); bus 217 to Hollywood/Las Palmas | Hours Daily
noon–8pm | Tip One block away is the Hollywood Museum in the historic Max Factor
building, where you can see the world's largest collection of Hollywood memorabilia
(1660 N Highland Avenue, www.thehollywoodmuseum.com).

87 Rooftop Movies
Cinema al fresco at the Montalbán

It's not surprising that there are plenty of good movie theaters in Hollywood. It's the home of the film industry, after all, so of course there are countless places where you can go see movies. They're mostly what you'd expect: velour seats, expensive concessions, lights off, movie magic. But there's no better way to see a movie than snuggled up outdoors under a blanket on a beautiful, cool Hollywood rooftop, sipping your favorite cocktail and munching a fresh popped bucket of popcorn or a delicious burger. Once you see a film atop the Montalbán Theatre, you may never want to go see movies inside again.

The Montalbán is named for the late great Mexican actor, Ricardo Montalbán, who is best remembered for his role as Mr. Roarke in the classic TV show *Fantasy Island*, and his turn as Khan in the *Star Trek* TV and movie franchise. But he also played dozens of roles that he found to be "caricatures," stereotyping Mexicans as seedy, criminal, and untrustworthy. He teamed with other Latinos in the industry to create an advocacy group called the Nosotros Foundation, and he served as its first president. The foundation, in partnership with Montalbán's own Montalbán Foundation, bought the Doolittle Theatre in 1999 and renamed it.

It's not the first name change for this beautiful Beaux-Arts theater. Since its inception in 1927, it has also been called the Wilkes' Vine Street Theatre, the Huntington Hartford Theatre, the Mirror Theatre, the Studio Theatre, and the CBS Radio Playhouse (aka Lux Radio Playhouse). Scores of high-profile productions have been staged there, featuring many A-list artists.

Be prepared to climb up a good number of stairs to reach the roof, but it's well worth the hike. The curated films are always on point, and with the bar, kitchen, and a collection of fun games to play, make sure you arrive well before showtime, and enjoy the sunset.

Address 1615 Vine Street, Hollywood, CA 90028, +1 (323) 871-2420, www.themontalban.com/rooftopmovies | **Getting there** Metro B to Hollywood/Vine (Red Line); bus 210 to Vine/Selma | **Hours** See website for screening schedule | **Tip** The fabulous Bourbon Room is around the corner. It's a great bar, and one of the best places in Hollywood to see live music (6356 Hollywood Boulevard, www.bourbonroomhollywood.com).

88 Runyon Canyon Park
Hiking with the stars

With Griffith Park at its edge, there's actually a good deal of great hiking right here in Hollywood. But one of the best hiking spots isn't actually in that storied park. There's a beautiful, 161-acre expanse of wilderness that's just west of the TCL Chinese Theatre, between Franklin and Mulholland Drive. It's by far the best place to see a celebrity out for a hike.

Runyon Canyon has been popular with the rich and famous for a long time, and you can wander through some of that history as you walk along the trail. Irish tenor John McCormack, who was world renowned a century ago, once owned this property and built a mansion here called San Patrizio, after Saint Patrick. After alimony payments forced the cinema heartthrob Errol Flynn out of his Hollywood Hills home, he too stayed here. By then, San Patrizio had been sold to Huntington Hartford, who renamed it "The Pines." He invited Flynn to stay in the pool pavilion, which had just been designed by Lloyd Wright. Flynn threw legendarily wild parties at the pavilion, and many locals falsely thought he owned the whole estate. The pavilion sadly burned down in 1972, but there are still some remnants of its foundation. There are plenty of other ruins along the path, including a giant neon sign from a housing development, tennis courts from an athletic compound, and more detritus from years of private use.

It's a lovely public city park now, where you can find outdoor yoga classes on the lawn at the bottom, so many impossibly beautiful people marching their way up and down, and a glorious view of Hollywood at the top. These attractions are undoubtedly why Katy Perry lived at the summit for a time.

A-listers are regularly spotted on the trails here, and, like everyone else sweating their way up the hill, they're often walking their dogs, who are allowed to be off leash in most areas. So watch your step.

Address 2000 N Fuller Avenue, Hollywood, CA 90046, +1 (818) 243-1145, www.laparks.org/runyon | Getting there By car, take Franklin Avenue and turn north on N Fuller Avenue | Hours Daily dawn–dusk | Tip After hiking with your dog, drop by the delicious Running Goose for a bite, where Fido is welcome to join you on the patio (1620 N Cahuenga Boulevard, www.runninggoose.weebly.com).

89   The Sapp Coffee Shop
Secret Thai food treasure

Even in death, the late Jonathan Gold remains the undisputed arbiter of culinary delights in Los Angeles. He is most well-known, perhaps, for all of the accolades and awards he received when he was above ground. After all, he was renowned for his food criticism in the venerable *Gourmet* magazine, not to mention *Rolling Stone* and *The Los Angeles Times*, to name only a few. Additionally, he was the first food critic ever to be awarded the Pulitzer Prize! But the real prize to be had was for the legions of eaters who followed his daring footsteps into the back alleys and strip malls of some of the grimiest corners of Los Angeles and elsewhere to discover the amazing and delicious treasures that always lay at the end of each scrumptious rainbow he described.

In 2003, his uncanny ability to track down delectable feasts in the unlikeliest of places led him into an awful, ugly, little strip mall in the heart of Hollywood's tiny Thai Town. He enjoyed the meal, and he wrote the review that put The Sapp Coffee Shop on the map.

Despite its name, Sapp Coffee Shop isn't a coffee shop at all. It is actually a wonderful hidden treasure of a Thai restaurant. How Gold stumbled upon it in the first place is a mystery, but one thing is certain: it's a good thing that the food is awesome. There are no frills to speak of, not much parking, and there's often a line of people waiting to get in. But none of those negatives should be an impediment to your visit.

Once you've eaten, you'll see the décor, the grittiness of the location, and the sometimes long wait as just the charming and quirky elements of the secret restaurant that Jonathan Gold "discovered" all those years ago. And although his grave marker at the Hollywood Forever Cemetery reads "Tacos Forever," you'll leave the Sapp Coffee House full of gratitude that Mr. Gold was a big fan of Thai food too.

Address 5183 Hollywood Boulevard, Hollywood, CA 90027, +1 (323) 665-1035, www.sappcoffeeshop.com, contact@sappcoffeeshop.com | Getting there Bus 180, 217 to Hollywood/Normandie | Hours Mon & Tue, Thu – Sun 8am – 6pm | Tip At the corner of Hollywood and Western stand two huge gilded statues of mythical, half-human, half-lion creatures welcoming visitors to the only designated "Thai Town" in the United States (Hollywood Boulevard and Western Avenue).

90 — Secret Stairways of Hollywoodland

Ascending to the stars

In 1923, the famous Hollywoodland sign went up to advertise the fancy new neighborhood below. These were lovely homes, and many of the stars of the next few decades, from Busby Berkeley to Humphrey Bogart to Bela Lugosi, lived here. There were stables and trails for horseback riding, and lots of sparkling swimming pools and tennis courts. This was a neighborhood for a life of leisure.

There's still a sense of whimsy and fun that makes the old Hollywoodland neighborhood in Beachwood Canyon well worth strolling through. And see if you can find the secret stairways here. These impossibly charming hidden staircases wind all over, connecting the neighborhoods and surprising those willing to put in the effort of finding and climbing with views of the Hollywood Sign, the Griffith Observatory, Lake Hollywood, and more. As you march up and down these narrow, shady stairways, it's easy to imagine what navigating this neighborhood was like before cars were common.

The staircases were built in a time when most people used public transit and needed to walk up the hill to their homes from where the streetcar stopped. The stone used to build many of the Hollywoodland secret stairs came from the nearby Bronson Quarry, also known as the Batcave. The result is a very hilly neighborhood that is impressively walkable.

Nowadays, most Angelenos have cars, but hiking the stairs is still popular. After all, it's great exercise, and the spectacular views are far better than anything you'll see in a gym. You'll see castles up there too, both literally and figuratively, as there are a few *actual* castles that are home to some big names in the movie business. And who knows? You may see some of their famous faces going up and down one of these secret stairways.

Address There are stairs throughout the neighborhood, start near 2748 Westshire Drive, Hollywood, CA 90068 | **Getting there** By car, from Franklin Avenue, drive north on N Beachwood Drive, and then right onto Westshire Drive | **Hours** Unrestricted | **Tip** A great place to stop for a coffee or a delicious meal before or after walking the stairs is The Beachwood Café (2695 N Beachwood Drive, www.beachwoodcafe.com).

91 Sexiest Loo in Hollywood

Pin-ups and Barry White

In an alley in the heart of Hollywood, you'll find a vintage garage sale full of great items from the 1970s. You may notice the distinct scent of marijuana wafting through the air as you browse through the funky clothing and psychedelic knick-knacks. Here, you can haggle over the price of that pair of hip huggers or the mug that says *#1 Dad* with a guy wearing a velvet blazer and yellow shades. You're sure to find some fun items to take home.

At the back of the garage, past the roller skates, eight-track tapes, and the smiley-face stickers, is an old refrigerator. Open the door, step *through* the fridge, and you'll be transported into a wood-paneled, midwestern-looking living room circa 1977, which is actually the front room of the popular 1970s themed bar Good Times at Davey Wayne's.

After enjoying one or two of the groovy beverages, like the "Jam Sesh" or the "Fat Elvis," and maybe a tequila sno-cone, you might need to find the bathroom. Stroll across the shag carpet, pass by the vintage cabinet doors used as wall tiles, and enter the coolest bathroom in Hollywood.

Like the rest of the bar, the room is detailed meticulously to feel like the house where the bar's owners, twins Mark and Jonnie Houston, grew up. By all appearances, it's clear these guys dig the Disco Era. "We had '70s décor til, like, the mid '90s," says Mark.

So perhaps it's the vintage pin-ups papering the walls – after all, this was the decade of Farrah Fawcett, Burt Reynolds, and Cheryl Tiegs. Or maybe it's the bodacious 1970s soundtrack with Donna Summer or Barry White heating up the dance floor just outside the door. Whatever the reason, the bathroom at Good Times at Davey Wayne's was anointed by OK Cupid daters as "The Best Bathroom for Sex in Los Angeles." (But just a reminder: just because it's called the best, having sex in the bathroom of a bar is definitely not cool.)

Address 1611 N El Centro Avenue, Hollywood, CA 90028, +1 (323) 498-0859, www.goodtimesatdaveywaynes.com, info@goodtimesatdaveywaynes.com | Getting there Metro B to Hollywood/Vine (Red Line) | Hours Thu–Sat, 8pm–2am, Sun 2pm–2am | Tip Less than a block away is the famous Amoeba Records. Check out live shows or just walk in and browse their world-class music collection (6200 Hollywood Boulevard, www.amoeba.com).

92 The Shakespeare Bridge

Idyllic hidden gardens

Local couples make a point of holding hands at sunset at the Shakespeare Bridge. Photoshoots to commemorate engagements, pregnancies, or proms often take place here. There's simply no denying that this is a romantic spot.

Thousands of cars drive over this picturesque bridge daily, and it's likely that many of them appreciate the charming gothic architecture that makes this part of Franklin Street so special. Some may have pulled over to read the plaque that commemorates the bridge's distinction as a Los Angeles cultural monument. But most of those drivers probably don't know that the best part of the Shakespeare Bridge, named, of course, for the famous playwright, is out of sight, hidden away in the shadows below.

It's not necessarily a good idea to go poking around under most bridges in Los Angeles, unless you're looking to discover trash, find feral animals, or to barge into someone's home. This bridge is no exception. Although this is an upscale part of town, where Roy and Walt Disney used to have homes next door to one another with an easy walk from the first Disney studios, the bridge had become an eyesore. It used to be covered with garbage, discarded drug paraphernalia, and other detritus of what seemed like a harrowing lifestyle for unhoused people who were living there. In an attempt to beautify the neighborhood and to push back against the unsightly rubbish that was piling up, some neighbors decided to plant a community garden underneath the bridge.

A little walk around the block reveals this secret garden. It isn't fancy, but it is lovingly tended by neighbors and beautiful all year round. There's a rumor that the bridge was used in the filming of the classic film *The Wizard of Oz*, but it's unconfirmed, and it's not easy to spot in the movie. It definitely did appear in the 1991 thriller *Dead Again*, but the gardens definitely disprove that title.

Address Franklin Avenue and St. George Street, Hollywood, CA 90027 | Getting there By car, take Franklin Avenue to St. George Street, turn left at Lyric Street, then left at Monon Street. The garden is at the end of the street. | Hours Unrestricted | Tip The Norman Harriton Community Garden of Franklin Hills can also be seen from the bridge, looking in the opposite direction from the Shakespeare garden (4155 Russell Avenue, www.facebook.com/ FranklinHillsCommunityGarden).

93 Snow White Cottages
Fairy tale home-sweet-home

In December of 1937, the Walt Disney corporation released its very first full-length animated movie, the beloved classic, *Snow White and the Seven Dwarfs*. It was an immediate success and is considered one of the most important animated films of all time, launching the global animation industry and establishing the empire of Disney. The movie is filled with all the sweet and silly imagery you'd expect from a Disney fairy tale: good and evil characters, soaring romantic landscapes, and of course, enchanting woodland creatures, all singing and frolicking around a quaint forest cottage.

The cute and delightful design of that little house in the woods, where seven dwarfs made a cozy home together amongst exceedingly cheerful critters, was inspired by real life, and those apartments still stand here at the edge of Hollywood. Just down the street from Disney's first studio, this charming chain of little cottages was built in 1931, to house employees for the burgeoning company in those early days. With whimsical, cartoonishly crooked roofs and patchy storybook brickwork around the window box planters, it's no wonder Disney used the look in the movie. Even the number of cottages, eight, seems a slightly suspicious coincidence. After all, once Snow White moved in, that was the exact number of residents.

Unsurprisingly, *Snow White and the Seven Dwarfs* isn't these cottages' only claim to fame. They have had many onscreen appearances, including being used prominently in David Lynch's mysterious 2001 paean to Hollywood, *Mulholland Drive*. Sadly, this is also the site of the 2003 stabbing murder of the songwriter Elliot Smith, who lived here before his demise, and whose murder is still unsolved. Despite that tragedy, these cottages still exude the playful feel of an animated forest in a sparkling fairy tale, where a cartoon romance may be just about to blossom.

Address 2900 Griffith Park Boulevard, Hollywood, CA 90027 | **Getting there** Bus 182 to St. George/Griffith Park | **Hours** Unrestricted from outside only | **Tip** Walk down St. George Street to see Marshall High School, where so many TV shows and hit movies were filmed, from *Grease* to *Pretty in Pink* to *Nightmare On Elm Street* (3939 Tracy Street).

94_The Spare Room
Bar that's not just playing around

The Spare Room isn't just another hipster Hollywood bar. On the contrary, this is a one-of-a kind, classy "gaming parlor," complete with two vintage bowling lanes and dozens of handcrafted board games. You might be playing checkers, Monopoly, or cribbage, but the luxury game appointments, carefully manicured setting, and custom cocktails will make your playtime anything but ordinary.

Located in the storied Hollywood Roosevelt Hotel, the Spare Room is filled, as you'd expect, with an unusual blend of whimsy and stylishness. After all, this is where so many actors lived when working on films in the Golden Age of Hollywood. Carole Lombard, Charlie Chaplin, Clark Gable and so many other legends stayed and played here. Marilyn Monroe lived here for two years and had her first professional photoshoot at the pool.

Even the cocktail menu is filled with fun. It's ever changing, but where else can you get a drink called "Birds Aren't Real" or "Bunny's Revenge"? If you're enjoying playing games, and you're feeling lucky, you might order the mysterious "Zoltar Vision" and "surrender your boozy fate to the Oracle," per the menu. Host a private party here, and you can even select a personalized drink menu.

It's not only the cocktails that are special, of course; all of the opulent amenities here are pretty unique. Case in point: If you decide to bowl, your "dedicated bowling attendant" will help fit you with custom, handmade shoes from an award-winning cobbler before grabbing an old-school chalkboard to keep score for you. They'll even offer you pointers on your bowling form, if you're open to that.

To preserve the memory of your time here, take a careful look around before you leave. Somewhere in the bar is a hidden photo booth. If you can find it, you can step in and get a beautiful black and white remembrance of your playful and posh night at the Spare Room.

Address 7000 Hollywood Boulevard, Hollywood, CA 90028, +1 (323) 769-7296,
www.spareroomhollywood.com, reservations@spareroomhollywood.com | Getting there
Metro B to Hollywood/Highland (Red Line); bus 212, 217 to Hollywood/Sycamore |
Hours Mon, Wed–Sat 8pm–2am | Tip Hollywood High School boasts beautiful murals
of Hollywood stars painted by Eloy Torrez. You'll see 13 famous faces, including Dolores del
Río, Selena, Laurence Fishburne, Rudolph Valentino, and more (1521 N Highland Avenue).

95 Stahl House

The case for Case Study Houses

The Stahl House, also known as "Case Study House #22," is an amazing, all-glass architectural wonder that has come to represent the mid-century modern aesthetic. It was immortalized by architectural photographer Julius Shulman, whose wonderful photos made the house famous and helped cement the modernist movement in America.

It all started in 1954, when Buck and Carlotta Stahl bought what was considered to be a dangerous and undesirable lot on a steep hill above Hollywood. Sure, it had a great view, but it was a precarious, rocky slope. It seemed crazy to build there, and the seller was delighted to be able to get rid of the property. But the Stahls had a vision. They happily paid a whopping $13,500 for the land. Buck spent a couple of years working on the lot himself, leveling a building site and making retaining walls, but they eventually brought in an architect in 1957. Pierre Koenig had studied with Richard Neutra and was an up-and-comer, who had just gotten involved in the "Case Study House Program," a project of *Arts and Architecture* magazine. Koenig had designed Case Study House #21, which is regarded as one of the best modernist homes ever built, and is also built on a difficult, steep lot.

The Stahl House, completed in 1960, is built from commercially available steel and glass. Being in some of the rooms here feels like you're soaring over Hollywood. Buck and Carlotta raised their three children there, who had no idea that they were living in such an important place. They roller skated all over the floors like any other kids. In 1999, the house was declared a Los Angeles Historic-Cultural Monument, and it remains one of the best examples of the mid-century modern movement. The house is still owned by the family, who live their daily lives inside this marvelous place, which is why you can only visit Stahl House on a tour – and why you have to make reservations in advance.

Address 1635 Woods Drive, Hollywood, CA 90069, +1 (208) 429-1058, www.stahlhouse.com |
Getting there By car, from Sunset Boulevard, drive north on Selma Avenue, left on N Crescent
Heights Boulevard, right on Hollywood Boulevard, left again on N Crescent Heights Boulevard,
then left onto Woods Drive. Stay to the left at the fork. | Hours Tours by reservation | Tip While
you're out enjoying amazing architecture, don't miss the Storer House, designed by Frank Lloyd
Wright (8161 Hollywood Boulevard, www.franklloydwright.org/site/john-storer-house).

96 Sunset Nursery
Generations of green thumbs

Greg Kuga grew up running around the potted plants crowding the aisles of the small but mighty Sunset Nursery, with the smell of rich soil and greenery. The nursery was started by his grandparents in the 1950s and remains the family-owned business it has always been. Residents of Hollywood, Silver Lake, and all the surrounding neighborhoods rely on the Sunset Nursery not only as a place to buy all the best indoor and outdoor plants, but also as a repository of knowledge. Whether you need to know how to tend your organic vegetables, or you've got a problem with an unruly bougainvillea, the friendly and knowledgeable staff here will set you right.

Kuga's father Dennis learned the nursery business from *his* father Bill who founded the Sunset Nursery not long after his internment at the Manzanar camp during World War II. In those early years at the nursery, there was a house on the property as well, and Bill lived and worked there with his young family, growing his business as carefully and lovingly as he grew his plants.

Some staff members have worked at the nursery for decades, and you quickly understand why. The sense of family and community here makes it easy to browse, ask questions, and leave with a whole lot of plants and projects, or just a scrap of key information about horticulture that you need. There's never any upselling or pressure, and maybe that's why it's become such a massively popular place to buy whatever your garden needs.

In the decades to come, it's easy to imagine the next generation of the Kuga family running and playing amongst the cacti and the vegetables and the gardenias and the ferns. And then one day, they'll pick up a watering can, a trowel, and a hose along with the mantle of the family business. Long live the green thumbs of the Kuga family, and long live the Sunset Nursery, your friendly neighborhood plant shop.

Address 4368 W Sunset Boulevard, Hollywood, CA 90029, +1 (323) 661-1642, www.sunsetboulevardnursery.com | Getting there Bus 2 to Fountain/Sunset | Hours Daily 9am–5pm | Tip Disney buffs will want to head over to take a look at the modest house that Walt Disney first lived in when he moved to Los Angeles (4406 Kingswell Avenue).

97 __ Sunset Ranch
Riding off into the sunset

The rugged terrain of Griffith Park is a reminder that this glitzy town is plunked down right at the edge of the American West, and tumbleweeds still blow through. So it shouldn't be a shock that there's a proper working dude ranch hidden away in these hills, where you can ride horses on the hundreds of miles of trails and bridle paths in the shadow of the Hollywood Sign.

Folks have been riding here since at least 1923, when it was home to the Hollywood Riding Club, formed to entice the wealthy to buy a home in the brand new Hollywoodland development. In 1952, it became Sunset Ranch, and it's still run by the descendants of its first owner, rodeo pro Jute Smith.

The ranch is a great place to celebrate a birthday or a proposal, and 1- or 2-hour rides are available 365 days a year (rain or shine) if you get to the ranch by 3pm; evening rides, including the epic 5-hour sunset dinner ride, are by reservation only. Beginners and experienced riders alike will enjoy one of the best views in Hollywood.

It's long been rumored that the ghost of a 16-year-old Mexican cowboy haunts the stables, having killed himself over his forbidden love for the daughter of a wealthy, white Hollywoodland resident. Sorry to burst your bubble, *Romeo & Juliet* fans, as that's not what happened. But the actual suicide that took place here was real and just as sad.

It turns out that back in 1921, Robert Bakefelt, a 43-year-old riding instructor from the old Hollywood Riding club, married Doris Langworth, who was half his age. She broke it off with him in 1923, and alas, he didn't take the news well. His 14-year-old son (from a previous marriage) returned from a walk to find his father hanging from the rafters. If you hear the distant terrible sounds of choking and the creaking of a rope, as some have reported, that's the reverberation of poor Robert, forlorn over losing his bride.

Address 3400 N Beachwood Drive, Hollywood, CA 90068, +1 (323) 469-5450, www.sunsetranchhollywood.com | Getting there By car, drive to the top of N Beachwood Drive | Hours See website for tour schedule | Tip Golfers will love the two award-winning 18-hole golf courses in Griffith Park, Wilson Golf Course and Harding Golf Course (5500 Griffith Park Drive, www.golf.lacity.org).

98__Tai Chi in the Park
Saturday morning calm in Bronson Park

In 1968, a local man named Marshall Ho'o founded Bronson Park Tai Chi. It's officially the Los Angeles chapter of the National Tai Chi Chuan Association (NTCCA), and Marshall was the perfect person for the role. He was not only a professor of Asian history at the California Institute of the Arts, but he also was the Chairman of the NTCCA. His influence in the martial arts community was vast: He'd been named as a member of *Black Belt* magazine's hall of fame and was widely regarded as a top master of the art of Tai Chi. So, teaching Tai Chi seemed natural. Marshall found a shady grove at Bronson Park and set about teaching and practicing Tai Chi every Saturday morning.

Although he passed in 1993 at age 83, his legacy lives on here in Hollywood. All these decades later, the group still meets in that little clearing every single Saturday, and for the cost of a small suggested donation, newcomers are welcome to join. Nobody is ever turned away. A couple of other leaders have stepped in through the years to fill the large void left by Ho'o, and they too were top masters of the form. And somehow, this little group has managed to keep going through earthquakes, fires, pandemics, and more. It makes sense that they've endured. Tai Chi is meant to promote focus and a feeling of being rooted to the ground, great skills to have in hard times. Beginners are welcome, and so are experienced practitioners. For experts, you'll want to know that this group practices the Yang form of Tai Chi Chuan.

You'll find a group every Saturday ready to welcome you into the practice, near the famous Batcave in Griffith Park. There's a tree that's been planted in memory of Marshall Ho'o, so while you're out there some Saturday morning, you can remember the roots of the small but mighty Tai Chi class that you're part of, and feel your feet on the ground and gratitude in your heart.

Address Bronson Canyon, 3200 Canyon Drive, Hollywood, CA 90068, www.taichila.com | Getting there By car, from Franklin Avenue, drive north on Canyon Drive | Hours Sat 8:30–11:30am | Tip This part of the park is home to the Cali Dance Camp, with affordable experiences at the historic Camp Hollywoodland for all ages, shapes and sizes (3200 Canyon Drive, www.danceengagements.org).

99 Temple Israel of Hollywood

Spiritual home for movie moguls

In 1926, some of the most prominent names in Hollywood's film industry founded Temple Israel. They were powerful people in the entertainment business, like titan producer Sol Wurtzel, who discovered Will Rogers and gave Marilyn Monroe her first role. There was prolific silent film director Edward Laemmle, whose uncle Carl founded Universal Studios. Screenwriter Isadore Bernstein, who wrote more than sixty successful films during the Silent Era, was one of the founders as well. The dozen or so first members of Temple Israel of Hollywood were basically some of the most well-connected guys in the industry.

So a few years later, when they were in fundraising mode to buy a building, and later to expand it, the founders decided to call their friends and put on a show to raise money. The first "Monster Midnight" show was in 1930. It ran for decades after, always with a star-studded cast. Over the years, names like Frank Sinatra, Judy Garland, Al Jolson, Lena Horne, Lucille Ball, and so many others lent their prodigious talents to the evening.

Martin Luther King famously spoke here in 1965, at a time when he hadn't ever been invited to speak at a temple in Los Angeles. The speech was only five days after the assassination of Malcolm X and was seen at the time as an important statement by the temple in support of Dr. King and the Civil Rights Movement in general.

The temple has grown over the years and now operates schools, programs that give back to the community, and regular services where all are welcome. You may even encounter a celebrity when you visit, as this is still a place whose congregation is dotted with famous faces. Leonard Nimoy was an active member for years, as were Sammy Davis, Jr. and Elizabeth Taylor. Nowadays, many well-known folks from all parts of the entertainment industry are members.

Address 7300 Hollywood Boulevard, Hollywood, CA 90046, +1 (323) 876-8330, www.tioh.org |
Getting there Bus 217 to Hollywood/Fuller | Hours See website for schedule of services and
events | Tip The Woman's Club of Hollywood is a local nonprofit doing good, and their beautiful
building has been designated as a cultural-historical monument (1749 N La Brea Avenue,
www.facebook.com/womansclubofhollywood).

100__ Theatre of NOTE

Expect the unexpected at the show that never ends

Founded in 1981 as a forum for one-act plays, Theatre of NOTE (New One-act Theatre Ensemble) has developed into a critically acclaimed company known for premiering outstanding, full-length, new work, as well as reinventing classic plays. Many well-known actors and playwrights cut their teeth here. Hollywood is most well-known for the movie business, obviously, but there's a thriving, vibrant theatre scene as well.

There's lots to say about the success of this theater, but let it suffice that this is a legitimate company with a stellar track record of meaningful, serious theatrical productions. However, if you showed up on marathon day, you'd think this was the wildest bunch of amazing lunatics you'd ever seen, putting on a show of such wide-ranging scope it would make your head spin. Want to see a tender folk song, followed by a pierced body suspension, followed by a Shakespearean monologue, followed by a fire eater, followed by a trombone solo? No problem, NOTE has got you covered.

The Theatre of NOTE Performance Marathon, featuring poetry, dance, mini plays, songs, harrowing stunts, and every kind of theatrical art imaginable, is all jammed into a much anticipated, annual, 24-hour performance mélange on the intimate, understated stage at this wonderful Hollywood venue.

It's not for everyone. You'll need a rather strong constitution, loads of patience, and some generosity of spirit. But if you love performance and you're in the mood for a roller coaster ride that includes some once-in-a-lifetime moments from the ridiculous to the sublime, you'll have the time of your life. So check the calendar, reserve your tickets, get yourself hydrated, and rest up because you'll need a lot of stamina for this all-day and all-night marathon of eclectic theatrical happenings. It's Theatre of NOTE's performance marathon, and it's a crazy scene.

Address 1517 N Cahuenga Boulevard, Hollywood, CA 90028, +1 (323) 856-8611,
www.theatreofnote.com | Getting there Bus 2 to Sunset/Ivar | Hours See website for
performance schedule | Tip Across the street is the Lighthouse Art Space, one of the most
immersive museums in Hollywood (6400 Sunset Boulevard, vangoghla.com).

101 The Three Clubs

Flashback to the Rat Pack

Upon approaching The Three Clubs, it's immediately clear you're not in the most glamorous part of Hollywood. This popular music venue and lounge is located in a dingy strip mall near the corner of Santa Monica and Vine, not exactly glitzy or glamorous. But once you've knocked on the door and the doorman peeking through the slider greets you speakeasy-style, you're transported.

With its leather banquettes, a black glitter ceiling, and a couple of stages with lounge acts from music to burlesque, The Three Clubs feels like a step back into 1950s Las Vegas. The Rat Pack vibe extends right down to the cocktail menu offering unfussy martinis and negronis, and the dress code. Don't try to wear shorts or sneakers here. There are no gangs of frat boys in flip flops to be found. It's not a pretentious place, but it's not casual either. This is where the smartly dressed step out.

The lounge opened back in 1991, and was already doing well by the time the iconic movie *Swingers* was being made in 1996. The film's writer and star Jon Favreau was a regular there, along with his co-star Vince Vaughn. The film didn't have much of a budget. Favreau's actual apartment was even used to shoot scenes meant to depict his character's apartment. To secure the use of the bar, they just asked if they could shoot where they were already regulars. While filming scenes here, the bar was actually open, and some of the people in the background of the film are actual bar patrons, not actors. The movie became a hit, and The Three Clubs, already a popular place, became even more of a hit as well.

That may help explain why celebrities are often seen here, and why, for a brief moment, there was a movie star behind the bar as well. Renée Zellweger used to be a barback here before she hit it big, and she has continued to be a customer even after finding fame and fortune.

Address 1123 Vine Street, Hollywood, CA 90038, +1 (323) 462-6441, www.threeclubs.com |
Getting there Bus 4, 210 to Santa Monica/Vine | Hours Daily 6pm–2am | Tip The Hollywood
Recreation Center is two blocks away and has the only public pool in the area, as well as
basketball courts and more (1122 Cole Avenue, www.laparks.org/reccenter/hollywood).

102 Trails Café
Destination: pastry

It doesn't look like much – just a rustic, unassuming, outdoor coffee stand with some picnic tables next to it. But once you're sitting in the lovely grove of trees, under the charming little string lights, scratching the ears of the happy dog that the conversational stranger sitting next to tells you they have just adopted, your outlook begins to change. The coffee is actually fantastic. The pie is unbelievably good, and you should not resist. The avocado sandwich is to die for. And the egg-in-a-basket? Just order it. Best of all, this whole idyllic and delicious scene is smack dab in the middle of the incomparable urban wilderness that is Griffith Park.

The wholesome little cabin that houses Trails Café is located near the Ferndell nature museum. Depending on the day of the week and time of day, you may see the long line of hikers waiting to order their lattes. It can take a few minutes to place your order, but, like many of life's good things, it's well worth the wait. A short walk up the road from Trails gets you to the start of a very nice hike up to the observatory, or to any number of different and wonderful spots in the massive park. If you're in the mood for a more leisurely stroll, the Batcave is nearby. Or simply walk in any direction, and you really can't go wrong following any trail you choose.

The café was founded in 2005 by Frank Lentz and Mickey Petralia, two Hollywood entertainment industry guys with zero experience running a café. No matter. They fixed it up, and folks began to flock there. But the real magic happened when pastry chef Jenny Park joined the team as a co-owner and brought a whole new level of scrumptiousness to the project. It's no surprise that loads of celebrities are spotted here savoring some of Park's delicious treats.

There are great spots all over Hollywood for al fresco snacks, but you'll be hard pressed to find one better for a pre- or post-hike nosh.

Address 2333 Fern Dell Drive, Hollywood, CA 90068, +1 (323) 871-2102, www.facebook.com/ TheTrailsCafe | Getting there By car, from Los Feliz Boulevard, enter the park on Fern Dell Drive, and drive until you see the café on your left | Hours Thu–Mon 8am–4pm | Tip There are so many treasures to discover in the park, such as the Mount Hollywood Tunnel near the Observatory. The tunnel is regularly used for filming including its role as the entrance to Toon Town in *Who Framed Roger Rabbit?* (Mount Hollywood Drive).

103 Travel Town

Train lovers' paradise

Long before Thomas the Tank Engine fascinated kids everywhere, Travel Town was a go-to destination for train lovers of all ages. It was founded in 1952, thanks to the inspiration of William Fredrickson, Jr., who was the superintendent of recreation in Los Angeles in the 1940s. Fredrickson wanted kids to be able to climb on board and explore retired military airplanes, and he managed to get one donated to Travel Town. Several planes, including a recovered Japanese fighter plane, were eventually added.

With Fredrickson's blessing, a Recreation and Parks employee named Charley Atkins made connections with some railroad enthusiasts and got an old train car donated. Thus were the wheels set in motion for this outdoor, hands-on train museum that's an absolute delight. More and more train cars were donated as the years went by, from the oldest steam engines to more modern models, and now there are dozens of trains to climb on and explore.

The aviation exhibits have all been moved to other museums, but everything train-related remains. Travel Town is run by the non-profit Travel Town Foundation, with a mission of education. To that point, there really is a lot to learn here about the history of railroads. But the genius of this place is that there is also a lot to do. There are lovely rides to take on the Travel Town Railroad, a miniature train that circumnavigates the museum. You can rent train cars or picnic areas for birthday parties, and there are numerous train-related exhibitions scattered all around the mostly open-air museum. All this is wonderful, but the real fun is in exploring all of the decommissioned, full-sized railroad cars. Climbing up and down the ladders of old engines, imagining meals in the dining cars, and hopping into boxcars will make even hardened cynics feel like kids again. Go for an hour or the whole day, or rent space for your next party.

Address 5200 Zoo Drive, Hollywood, CA 90027, +1 (323) 668-0104, www.traveltown.org | Getting there By car, from Crystal Springs Drive, turn onto Griffith Park Drive, which becomes Zoo Drive | Hours Daily 10am–5pm | Tip Right next to Travel Town is the Los Angeles Live Steamers Railroad Museum where you can ride a tiny steam-powered train (5202 Zoo Drive, www.lalsrm.org).

104 The Tropicana Pool

Swim in a David Hockney painting

David Hockney is world famous for his iconic paintings of Southern California swimming pools. Mostly created in the 1960s and 1970s, the paintings can make you almost feel the bright sunlight on your skin, and they mesmerize with their images of uninhibited swimmers in dancing swirls of rippling water. With their bold, vivid colors and sensuous subjects, some of the paintings seem to beckon the viewer to dive right in – it looks like that would be pretty darn wonderful.

There aren't many places where you can turn the feeling of diving in and swimming in a David Hockney painting into a reality. The Tropicana Pool at the Roosevelt Hotel might be the only place in the world to pull it off. Hockney painted the pool mural there in 1988, but it perfectly complements the Tropicana Café's 1960s décor. The entire bottom of the pool itself is covered in bold, blue strokes, like a thousand whimsical bits of blue macaroni. The moment the water is disturbed by a swimmer or even a stiff breeze, the noodles of color turn into those playful Hockney ripples, turning the pool into a painting and the painting to a pool. There's that feeling that you want to jump right in – and now you can!

Even setting aside the amazing pool mural, this spot is rich with history that you can almost feel. Celebrities often have parties here after movie premieres, and any day of the week, there might be an exciting event that draws out Hollywood's elite. Marilyn Monroe did her very first photo shoot here in 1951, posing on the diving board. She also lived in a cabana above the bar for a couple of years, and Clark Gable lived here too.

Even if you're not a hotel guest, anyone can dine in the fabulous Tropicana Café. Take a journey into the world of a David Hockney painting with a refreshing cocktail and bite of delicious food, and soak in the ambiance of a shrine to Old Hollywood.

Address 7000 Hollywood Boulevard, Hollywood, CA 90028, +1 (323) 466-7000, www.thehollywoodroosevelt.com/about/food-drink/tropicana-pool-cafe | Getting there Metro B to Hollywood/Highland (Red Line) | Hours Daily 7am–7pm | Tip Hollywood is filled with public art of all kinds. Take a walk to Columbia Square and check out *Psychogeographies* by Dustin Yellin (6121 W Sunset Boulevard, www.publicartinpublicplaces.info/psychogeographies-2015-by-dustin-yellin).

105 __ Upright Citizens Brigade

Taking comedy seriously

It all began in 1993 in Chicago, where the original cast of the Upright Citizens Brigade (UCB) performed sketches and improv to adoring crowds. The performers were a bunch of young, silly folks nobody had ever heard of, like Adam McKay. Yes, *that* Adam McKay, who is now known as one of the hottest writers and directors in Hollywood, with a collection of Academy Awards, BAFTAs, and Golden Globes cluttering his trophy case. Another unknown artist in the founding cast was Amy Poehler, who has become a household name as one of the funniest and most successful comic actors of a generation, and who has her own star on the Hollywood Walk of Fame.

The ragtag band of nobodies who would go on to be A-listers moved Upright Citizens Brigade to New York a few short years after their Chicago launch. After much success there as well, they opened in Hollywood in 2005. It's a vibrant and hilarious place. You can take classes and workshops, offered year round, and enjoy acclaimed performances featuring students, teachers, and alumni.

There are a multitude of other comedy groups out there, of course. But the Upright Citizens Brigade is the only performance troupe that is also an accredited institution of improvisation and sketch comedy instruction. This distinction may sound funny, as this place is all about laughter, after all. But in fact, the UCB Theatre and Training Center is serious business. Some extremely talented people, like Poehler, helped design the curriculum, which has a proven track record. In addition to those who have become celebrities, some of the UCB alumni have gone on to be writers for *Saturday Night Live*, Jimmy Fallon, Key and Peele, and many other hit TV and film productions.

Low ticket prices and ample shows make this place accessible and fun. Performances happen regularly, and any of the funny folks you see on any given night could be a big star tomorrow.

Address 5919 Franklin Avenue, Hollywood, CA 90028, www.ucbcomedy.com, tickets@ucbcomedy.com | Getting there Bus DASH Hollywood to Franklin/Bronson | Hours See website for performance schedule | Tip Birds is a fabulous bar and restaurant right next to the UCB theater. Stop in for food and drinks before or after the show (5925 Franklin Avenue, www.birdshollywood.com).

106 The Vedanta Temple
Hollywood's secret Taj Mahal

When people hear the word Hollywood, it usually conjures up a sparkling image from the movies: glamorous stars gliding down the red carpet, dressed to the nines, or perhaps a bustling movie set, buzzing with activity. Most don't associate Tinseltown with spirituality and the quiet practices of religious life.

The truth is that Hollywood has a rich spiritual and religious history, going all the way back to the 19th century. Unbeknownst to most visitors and locals as well, right next to the Hollywood Freeway is an incredibly charming temple of the Vedanta Society, complete with a dome and finial resembling the architecture of the Taj Mahal. It's tucked away behind the sound barrier and vegetation of the freeway, where it can be a haven of peacefulness and calm. There's a monastery and a convent here, filled with friendly people. The bookstore and worship services are open to the public.

The story of how the temple came to be here dates back to a single important believer and patron. In the 1890s, Swami Vivekananda traveled from India to visit Los Angeles, where he was hosted by the Mead sisters in South Pasadena. One of the sisters, Carrie Mead Wyckoff, was so moved by the teachings of the swami that 30 years later, when Swami Prabhavananda, another Vedanta monk, visited, she gifted him with a house that she owned in Hollywood. By 1929, the Vedanta Society of Southern California was made official, and in 1938, Mrs. Wyckoff had donated enough money to build the exquisite temple you can visit today.

The Vedanta Society has grown in popularity over time. There are now temples and centers all over North America, and across the world as well. But one of the loveliest places to experience the peaceful community remains the Hollywood temple, quietly resting in the chaos and bustle around it, waiting to be discovered by those who seek an oasis of calm.

Address 1946 Vedanta Place, Hollywood, CA 90068, +1 (323) 465-7114, www.vedanta.org, hollywood@vedanta.org | Getting there By car, from Franklin Avenue, turn north onto Argyle Avenue, left at Vine Street, left at Vedanta Terrace to Vedanta Place. | Hours Daily 6:30–8am, noon–1:15pm, 6–7pm, Sun 11am–1:15pm | Tip Kettle Glazed Doughnuts, a short walk away, offers a different kind of religious experience (6211 Franklin Avenue, www.kettleglazed.com).

107 — Was ist das?

Old-timey cabaret in the front yard

In Helene Udy's modest front yard on the Eastern edge of Hollywood, things are a little different. There's a crowd of people, laughing and crying, cheering, singing, and drinking, but it's not a barbeque or a birthday party. In this unusual yard, the only one on the street adorned with giant red curtains, lights, microphones, and a tiny stage, there's something going on that is truly unique in Hollywood and beyond. In Helene's yard one evening, you are whisked back to 1924, and you are in a smoky club in Berlin, at a cabaret show that's part circus, part concert, part burlesque, and all delightful.

This peculiar time machine that transports us back to a raucous spectacle filled with clowns, puppets, magicians, acrobats, raunchy jokesters, and musicians is a show that Helene and her rotating band of performers present every month. People flock to this residential neighborhood from all around Los Angeles to see the "utter comedy and daring acts" that are promised. Neighbors walking their dogs stroll by and pause on the sidewalk to take in the exploits that are hilarious, heartrending, bizarre, or some amazing combination of all three.

Sure, there are plenty of other performances happening in Hollywood on any given night, but this slapdash variety show has a homemade charm that feels a bit like the neighborhood kids all got together in someone's backyard to put on a scrappy play that they just invented. And these performers are pretty darn talented. Even the weather can't stop them. On infrequent rainy days, the whole cabaret moves inside the house, which, it must be noted, is even more charming than the yard.

So, to answer the question posed by the show's title, *Was ist das?* It's a little bit hard to say for sure, but one thing is very clear: it's a very eclectic, unique, and enjoyable way to spend an unforgettable evening under Hollywood skies.

Address 5000 Franklin Avenue, Hollywood, CA 90027, +1 (323) 687-0919, www.facebook.com/wasistdasshow, wasistdasshow@gmail.com | Getting there Bus DASH Hollywood to Franklin/Edgemont or Franklin/Normandie | Hours See website for performance schedule | Tip Find your inner peace with a visit to the Kadampa Meditation Center, a Buddhist Temple in the neighborhood (4953 Franklin Avenue, www.meditateinla.org).

108 Wattles Mansion
Lovely "Jualita" from a bygone age

If you're trying to find one of the very first tourist attractions in Hollywood, you need to look no further than the beautiful Wattles Mansion. Gurdon Wattles had this stunning estate built in 1913, not only as a winter home to escape the frigid climes of Omaha, but also to serve as an inspiring reminder of his trips to exotic locales. He covered the nearly 50-acre parcel with lush, themed gardens, carving beautiful scenes into the landscape evoking his favorite parts of Mexico and Japan. He imported lanterns and even an entire teahouse from Japan to complete his vision. The orchards full of avocados, citrus, and other delights teemed with fruit, the gardens thrived, and folks flocked to see all of the splendor. The estate was nicknamed "Jualita," and it was the talk of the town.

Wattles wasn't the only Midwesterner drawn to what was then a largely agricultural area. In fact, Hollywood was once the go-to spot for wealthy people from the eastern and midwestern states to winter. These days, however, the mansion and gardens of Wattles Park are perhaps the only remaining examples from Hollywood's pre-film years, when giant estates of wintering snowbirds were plentiful.

In the 1960s, the Wattles family sold the estate to the city, and it sat decaying and largely neglected for a couple of decades. The teahouse in the Japanese gardens became a popular spot for junkies to shoot up, and most of it burned down in a fire. But a restoration project for the mansion began in the 1980s. With time and care, lovely Jualita emerged once more and was designated as a cultural monument in 1993.

Nowadays, the fancy gardens have become a four-acre community garden, where locals tend to vegetables and flowers. The estate is popular with runners and walkers, and the mansion – once voted the best wedding spot in town – can be rented for weddings or other events.

Address 1824 N Curson Avenue, Hollywood, CA 90046, +1 (323) 969-9106, www.laparks.org/historic/wattles-mansion-and-gardens | Getting there By car, from Hollywood Boulevard, drive north on N Curson Avenue | Hours Tue–Fri noon–4pm, Sat 9am–3pm | Tip Movie buffs and celebrity home fans should take the short walk from Wattles Mansion to the last residence of Orson Welles (1717 N Stanley Avenue).

109__ The Wisdom Tree
The Phoenix of Griffith Park

In May of 2007, Hollywood residents were stunned to look up toward their beloved Griffith Park, one of the largest urban parks in the world (sorry New York, but five Central Parks would fit inside Griffith), and see that it was engulfed in flames. Southern California is quite accustomed to wildfires, but not right in the heart of town! The conflagration burned 817 lush acres of the iconic park, and when the smoke finally cleared, there at the top of Burbank peak stood one surviving majestic pine, lovingly known as The Wisdom Tree.

Most weekends, a steady stream of hikers and trail runners make their sweaty ascent to bask in the wide-open arms of this magnificent tree. The hike is challenging but under two miles long, and intrepid walkers are well rewarded for their toil up the steep trail. At the summit is an expansive, 360-degree view. Look for Burbank to the North and Hollywood to the South, and on a clear day, you can see all the way out to Catalina Island. There's an American flag flying nearby that was placed to commemorate the events of September 11th, 2001.

Nestled around the base of the tree is a treasure trove of "words of wisdom" in the form of notes and offerings from previous visitors. Take the time to peruse the box filled with the notebooks, drawings, jokes, and wishes that were left by others, and bring your own pen and paper to leave your legacy for the next hiker who is willing to scramble up the rocky trail.

One bit of wisdom left by a thoughtful idealist encapsulates the spirit of adventure and exploration necessary to reach this perch. "Follow your heart, not your pocketbook. At the end of the day, wealthy with memories, you'll realize that you don't need to be the richest man in the graveyard." The day you make your pilgrimage to the Wisdom Tree will undoubtedly be valuable enough to keep safe in the memory bank.

Address Atop Burbank peak in Griffith Park, 4730 Crystal Springs Drive, Hollywood, CA 90027, +1 (323) 644-2050, www.laparks.org/griffithpark/griffith-park-home-page | Getting there By car, drive to Cahuenga Boulevard, left on Barham Boulevard, turn right on Lake Hollywood Drive, then a 1.6-mile hike to the summit and back | Hours Unrestricted | Tip Griffith Park has miles of wonderful hiking trails. Continue along the ridge instead of heading back down the hill, and you'll arrive at the back of the Hollywood Sign, where you can see the impressive support structures, not to mention the view of the city below.

110_ The Woods

Ganja giggle garden

Hollywood has been on the leading edge of all kinds of progress, so when marijuana was legalized for recreational use in California in 2016, it was only natural that pot shops began to pop up all over to serve the suddenly out-in-the-open needs of the community. But it wasn't until 2022 that a cannabis lounge, complete with private cabanas in a lush, 5,000-square-foot garden, elevated smoking weed to the luxurious heights that Hollywood deserves. Yes, these are high heights.

There are convenient curbside pickup and delivery options from both the "recreational" and "medicinal" menus at The Woods, but you'd be missing out on the experience and the ambiance of the outdoor lounge. The koi pond and beautiful gardens are an oasis, complete with filtered, climate-controlled air in the cabanas and just the right amount of chill vibes emanating from the charming staff and increasingly buoyant customers. There's a fire pit and a tropical, tiki-lounge sensibility, complete with several actual parrots, some of whom have their own Instagram pages. Although it can't be smoked, the well-maintained jungle of greenery offers a sense of peace and well-being. The lovely design of the place is by the Shoos Design, who are responsible for many notable locations in New York, Las Vegas, Los Angeles, and more.

One of the co-owners of this "ganja giggle garden," as they call it, is movie star and one of Hollywood's biggest pot enthusiasts, Woody Harrelson. He's not shy about his participation in this upscale dispensary/lounge. A promotional photo for The Woods features a much younger, shirtless Harrelson holding a joint and looking like he's sitting on a cloud. It's appropriate because spending an hour or two in a cannabis cabana in the garden at The Woods, enjoying the high-end tonics, edibles, and smokables from the dispensary may well leave you floating on a cloud of your own.

Address 8271 Santa Monica Boulevard, West Hollywood, CA 90046, +1 (844) 484-3966, www.thewoodsweho.com, info@thewoodsweho.com | Getting there Bus 2, 4 to Santa Monica/ Sweetzer | Hours Mon–Thu 1–11pm, Fri & Sat 1pm–1am | Tip Munchies? No problem. Don't Touch My Cookies offers curbside pickup of their many varieties of fresh-baked artisanal chocolate chip beauties (1006 N Sierra Bonita Avenue, www.donttouchmycookies.com).

111 __ The World of Illusions

Smash your troubles away

Hollywood is known to be a town in which image is everything. The way that people and things are presented and, of course, the way they are perceived, is critical. So it makes sense that there would be a museum here that plays around with the very idea of image and offers up a way to bend reality until it's hard to know what to believe. Welcome to the World of Illusions.

Most of the museum is harmless, playful, and, well, nonviolent. There are all kinds of 3-D illusions to wander through here, and it's a lot of fun to take unbelievable photos of yourself in some amazing scenes. First, you'll be stuck on the window ledge way up a skyscraper. Next, you'll be in an upside-down house, where everything is topsy-turvy. The giant's house will shrink you to the size of a mouse, and you'll see what it's like to have to navigate the enormous world.

But the real treasure here is in the "Smash It!" room, where you can take out all of your real-world frustrations in a very physical experience. This room is extremely interactive, and not just in a selfie-taking kind of way. You'll be provided with plates and other destructible objects for your session, as well as protective gear. And then, like The Hulk says, *smash!*

You don't need to be a rage-a-holic to enjoy this place. Perhaps there are simply some things in your personal or professional life that you'd like to get rid of or transcend. The staff here will be happy to give you a marker so that you can take a stack of dishes and write something on them so that each and every dish represents something personal. Then throw it hard, and let the catharsis begin. Smash It! is a safe and fun way to release the destructive feelings that may have been growing inside of you for a while. Leave those angry or frustrated thoughts in pieces on the floor of Smash It! And let the image of you, as a more peaceful person, emerge into a new day.

Address 6751 Hollywood Boulevard, Hollywood, CA 90028, +1 (800) 593-2902, www.laillusions.com, infola@bigfunnyusa.com | Getting there Metro B to Hollywood/ Highland (Red Line); bus 212, 217, 224 to Hollywood/Highland | Hours Daily 11am–10pm | Tip If you like hard to believe illusions, stroll four blocks down to Black Rabbit Rose and take in an amazing magic show (1719 N Hudson Avenue, www.blackrabbitrose.com).

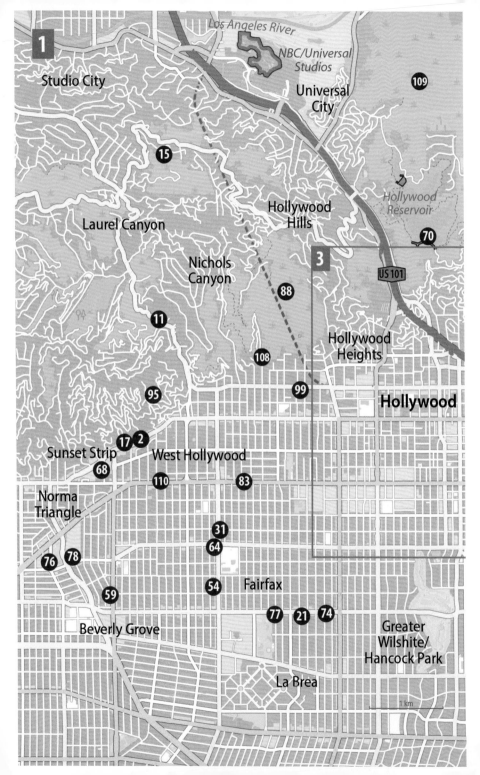

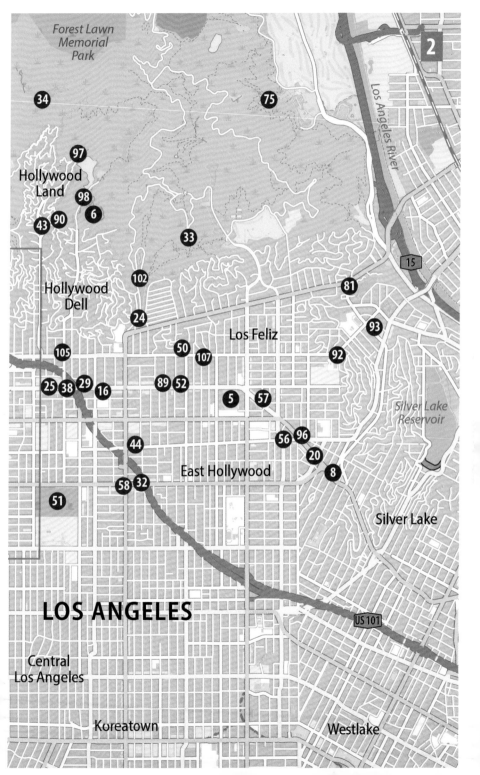

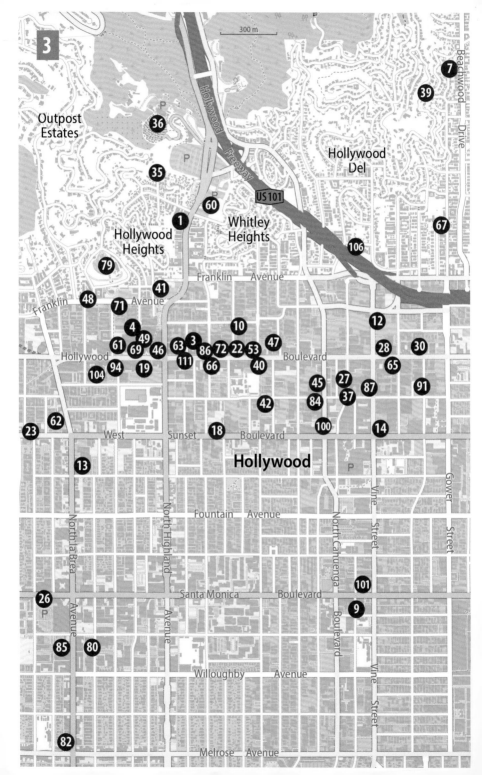

Laurel Moglen, Julia Posey,
Lyudmila Zotova
111 Places in Los Angeles
That You Must Not Miss
ISBN 978-3-7408-1889-0

Floriana Petersen, Steve Werney
111 Places in San Francisco
That You Must Not Miss
ISBN 978-3-7408-1698-8

Floriana Petersen,
Steve Werney
111 Places in Silicon Valley
That You Must Not Miss
ISBN 978-3-7408-1346-8

Katrina Nattress, Jason Quigley
111 Places in Portland
That You Must Not Miss
ISBN 978-3-7408-0750-4

Harriet Baskas, Cortney Kelley
111 Places in Seattle
That You Must Not Miss
ISBN 978-3-7408-1992-7

Kelsey Roslin, Nic Yeager,
Jesse Pitzler
111 Places in Austin
That You Must Not Miss
ISBN 978-3-7408-1642-1

Dana DuTerroil, Joni Fincham,
Daniel Jackson
111 Places in Houston
That You Must Not Miss
ISBN 978-3-7408-1697-1

Dana DuTerroil, Joni Fincham,
Sara S. Murphy
111 Places for Kids in Houston
That You Must Not Miss
ISBN 978-3-7408-1372-7

Philip D. Armour, Susie Inverso
111 Places in Denver
That You Must Not Miss
ISBN 978-3-7408-1220-1

Cristyle Egitto, Jakob Takos
111 Places in Palm Beach
That You Must Not Miss
ISBN 978-3-7408-1695-7

Jo-Anne Elikann, Susan Lusk
111 Places in New York
That You Must Not Miss
ISBN 978-3-7408-1888-3

Kim Windyka, Heather Kapplow,
Alyssa Wood
111 Places in Boston
That You Must Not Miss
ISBN 978-3-7408-1558-5

Andréa Seiger, John Dean
111 Places in Washington
That You Must Not Miss
ISBN 978-3-7408-1890-6

Brandon Schultz, Lucy Baber
111 Places in Philadelphia
That You Must Not Miss
ISBN 978-3-7408-1376-5

Allison Robicelli, John Dean
111 Places in Baltimore
That You Must Not Miss
ISBN 978-3-7408-1696-4

Amy Bizzarri, Susie Inverso
111 Places in Chicago
That You Must Not Miss
ISBN 978-3-7408-1030-6

Michelle Madden, Janet McMillan
111 Places in Milwaukee
That You Must Not Miss
ISBN 978-3-7408-1643-8

Sandra Gurvis, Mitch Geiser
111 Places in Columbus
That You Must Not Miss
ISBN 978-3-7408-0600-2

Gratitude is due to so many people who helped me with this book. To Karen, my editor and fellow runner who helped me cross the finish line. To Julia Posey, who told me about this series and bugged me to get involved. To my sister Diana for honest proofreading and constant support. Griffin, Ravi, Lila Rose, and Rowan, who make everything better. Much appreciation to friends and family members who made suggestions, and who have had to listen to me yammer on about Hollywood for ages. Lastly, thanks to everyone I met at each of these 111 places. Your enthusiasm for these spots was contagious, and I'm glad I caught it. Most of all, thank you to my partner Susan, who encourages even my craziest ideas, and makes the dubious claim to still love me after all these years, in spite of all my nonsense.

 **Brian Joseph** is an artist whose work has been shown in galleries and private collections internationally. In addition to making photographs, he also makes songs, stories, very tasty lasagna, children, and crossword blunders. He can be found sipping coffee on the east side of Los Angeles with his two dogs, four kids, and one fantastic wife. www.brianjosephunlimited.com

The information in this book was accurate at the time of publication, but it can change at any time. Please confirm the details for the places you're planning to visit before you head out on your adventures.